Warman's

Costume JEWELRY

IDENTIFICATION AND PRICE GUIDE

Pamela Y. Wiggins

PHOTOGRAPHY BY

Jay B. Siegel

Published by

Krause Publications, a division of F+W Media, Inc.
700 East State Street • Iola, WI 54990-0001
715-445-2214 • 888-457-2873
www.krausebooks.com

To order books or other products call toll-free 1-800-258-0929
or visit us online at www.krausebooks.com

Front cover: Elizabeth Taylor "Eternal Flame" earrings, c. 1993, marked Elizabeth Taylor Avon, 1 5/8" long, $150-$200; Joseff of Hollywood tassel brooch, c. 2000s, marked Joseff, 6 3/4" long, $500-$650; Chanel Gripoix cuff bracelet, c. 1980s, marked Chanel 2 CC 5 Made in France, 2 1/2" wide, $6,000-$6,500 (courtesy ChicAntiques.com)

Back cover: Regency bracelet, c. 1950s, marked Regency, 7" long, $125-$150; Mimi Di N geometric brooch, c. 1960s, marked Mimi Di N, 3 1/4" wide, $200-$250 (courtesy LinsyJsJewels.com)

Spine: Schreiner brooch, c. 1950s, marked Schreiner New York, 3 7/8" long. $225-$275

Inside back cover: Author photo: Jennifer Jones, Luxe Photography; DeLizza & Elster parure, c. 1960s, $1,100-$1,300

ISBN-13: 978-1-4402-3944-1
ISBN-10: 1-4402-3944-4

Designed by Nicole MacMartin
Edited by Mary Sieber
Cover Designed by Jana Tappa and Nicole MacMartin

Printed in China

10 9 8 7 6 5 4

Table of CONTENTS

To my late mother, Eva Paschal, with whom I shared many wonderful collecting adventures.

ACKNOWLEDGEMENTS

There are so many people who have helped me and encouraged me on my jewelry-collecting journey that it's impossible to list them all here. Many of these wonderful folks are friends of Costume Jewelry Collectors International, an organization for collectors my great friend Melinda Lewis and I co-founded. I appreciate everything I've learned from all of you and the jewelry experiences we've shared over the years with many more to come.

And, of course, I have to give my partner Jay Siegel a very special thank you for everything he contributed, from encouragement to photography to editing, and most of all patience and love, to make sure this book came together on schedule. There's really nothing in the world like having a life partner you love who is also a talented and supportive work partner.

INTRODUCTION

"One should either be a work of art, or wear a work of art." – Oscar Wilde

I love this quote from the inimitable Oscar Wilde, and I wholeheartedly agree. Since most of us don't consider ourselves to be works of art, we should definitely be wearing them. Jewelry, whether old or new, certainly offers an unparalleled way to enhance self-expression. But collectible jewelry takes the notion one step further when design, artistry, and craftsmanship come together to create works of art we not only admire but enjoy wearing as well.

My introduction to vintage costume jewelry came when I purchased a few pieces at an estate sale while shopping with my mother. This was about 25 years ago. I wasn't looking for jewelry. It was colorful old glass that drove my hunting and gathering instinct back then. And after growing up in my mom's antiques shop, I already knew a lot more about antiques and collectibles than most folks twice my age. My time spent working for department stores like Sakowitz and Saks Fifth Avenue had also helped me develop a fondness for stylish adornment, so I did recognize quality even if I wasn't well-versed in vintage jewelry just yet.

I took a chance and purchased two necklaces and a brooch that seemed pretty nice at first glance. One of my co-workers was also a glass fan, and when I mentioned that I had found some jewelry I was interested in researching, she traded me a copy of Lillian Baker's first book on costume jewelry for a set of Fire King mixing bowls I purchased at the same estate sale. It turned out those first jewelry buys were Miriam Haskell pieces. Baker's book told me I had some real treasures on my hands. I'd purchased them for $1 apiece.

This was long before the Internet opened up a whole new world for collectors. We were still doing things the "hard way" back then. I sold those first Haskell buys through a classified ad placed in *Antique Trader*, bought a few more pieces here and three, started keeping favorites for myself, bought every book I could find on the topic, joined an organization for jewelry collectors, and never looked back except to thank my lucky stars that I stopped at that estate sale right there in the neighborhood where I grew up in Houston, Texas.

Since then I've bought and sold literally thousands of pieces of collectible jewelry. I've started two local jewelry collecting clubs, and co-founded an international organization called Costume Jewelry Collectors International (CJCI) with my Napier-collecting buddy, Melinda Lewis, and together we host annual events for jewelry collectors and provide educational resources online. I also obtained a journalism degree and began writing about antiques and collectibles along the way, always relishing the opportunity to expound on jewelry topics whenever possible.

Today, a good part of my life revolves around collectible jewelry. I've had the opportunity to meet and interview Kenneth Jay Lane. I visited with Lawrence Vrba who designed for Miriam Haskell and Castlecliff in his grand New York studio. I met Patricia Ciner Hill and enjoyed poring over the jewelry in the Ciner showroom where many vintage styles are still sold alongside new ones. The list chronicling my costume jewelry obsession and related adventures goes on and on. But what's even more important is continuously buying, selling, researching, writing, evaluating, appraising, wearing, and discussing all types of jewelry through numerous venues. To say I love this stuff and can't get enough of it could easily be deemed a gross understatement.

I'm also adamant about dispelling costume jewelry myths when I can, documenting history as accurately as possible at any given time, and even supporting those who are rewriting history as new information is uncovered. You can find many of the resources I've developed for collectors and others I've assisted in developing on www.costumejewelrycollectors.com and on my About.com site at www.antiques.about.com. I'm also honored to be carrying on the Warman's tradition of educating collectors by putting together this book.

Champagne glass brooch, c. 1960s, brushed gold with simulated pearl "bubbles" and clear rhinestone accents, unmarked, just over 2 5/8" long. **$65-$95**

Author's Collection

Does this mean I'm an "expert" on collectible costume jewelry? By the average person's standards, the answer would be yes. I know a good bit about these old baubles and I make new discoveries daily as I continue my study. Are there people out there who know more than I do about various jewelry-related topics and designers? I can say, wholeheartedly, yes. But what makes me uniquely qualified to write this book – in addition to being a professionally trained and experienced journalist who knows how to research just about any topic under the sun – is passion. I wouldn't dedicate so much of my personal and professional life to costume jewelry pursuits if I didn't have a real fire in the gut for beautiful, intriguing jewelry of all kinds.

So as you peruse these pages and view many of the pieces I have collected over time or owned during the past few years before passing them on to others, along with a number borrowed from friends who love collectible jewelry as much as I do, remember the words that go along with them are carefully chosen not only to educate, but to whet your appetite about each decade, designer, manufacturer, and style so you're encouraged to seek out even more information on your favorites, just as I have. And at the very least, I believe you'll walk away with an ample introduction to the world of collectible costume jewelry and an accurate guide you can rely on for future reference.

ABOVE, TOP Miriam Haskell brooch, c. 1940s, filigree ribbon flower with rose montee rhinestones, marked Miriam Haskell, 2 3/4" wide. **$450-$575**

Jewelry courtesy LinsyJsJewels.com

ABOVE Ciner earrings, c. 1960s, sapphire blue and ruby red rhinestones accented by simulated turquoise beads, marked Ciner, 1" long. **$100-$125**

Jewelry courtesy ChicAntiques.com

Why You Need This Book

One of the things we know for certain is that many people will never "get" costume jewelry collecting. They see a pile of rhinestones and think "junk" when a true collector sees potential for beauty in the wearing, artistry in the design, and history hidden in the style and components. There are other folks who have a curiosity about trinkets they've inherited or were given by a friend, and they have no real clue that what they own might be historically significant or worth something since it has little intrinsic value in comparison to fine jewelry. And, of course, collectibles dealers have a real need to learn about these pieces so they can market them appropriately.

This book is designed to serve a number of audiences with an interest in vintage and collectible jewelry, whether they're just trying to find out if the goodies in Grandma's jewelry box should go to a high-end auction house or be donated to the local thrift store. It serves as a tool for dating many pieces as well, whether the owner is contemplating selling them or just wants the satisfaction of knowing a little something about the objects she holds dear. It will also help collectors – especially beginners and those with moderate experience – grade and classify the things they've amassed. Even old-timer collectors will likely learn something new, and they'll certainly appreciate how important it is for a good overall book on jewelry to include many of the basics required to get collectors off to a great start.

As often as possible, a bit of history behind the pieces shown in this book will be shared to encourage appreciation in terms of how they were worn in the past, as well as interesting tidbits that transform mere adornments into wearable conversation pieces. This equates to manufacturing information, interjections about designers where known, and how trends and pop culture influenced fashion and jewelry production through the decades.

This guide also serves to dispel some myths widely circulated about vintage jewelry that were previously published in other books. Some of these misnomers were honest mistakes made by authors with good intent; others were fairly significant assumptions that turned out to be false and were inadvertently perpetuated with verve. As costume jewelry historians did further research after the information was originally published, whether in print or online, they found clues that brought those errors to light. In other cases, interviews with jewelry manufacturers and in-depth research failed to substantiate assumptions. Pointing out these errors isn't meant to discredit the much-appreciated and oftentimes valuable work and research done by others, but rather to right the wrongs that can so easily become accepted as fact over time as they're repeated again and again. This happens with other types of "history" books, so it stands to reason collectibles books will become outdated over time as new information is discovered.

This is especially true for costume jewelry marketers who aren't active in communities where these types of errors are fervently discussed. They refer to older books because that's what they have in their libraries, not realizing the information they're sharing with customers is incorrect. And, unfortunately, sometimes they just don't care. They just want to turn a quick buck so they use keywords to garner interest in their wares, like "runway," "haute couture," and "Hollywood Regency" to attract buyers when those terms may not truly be applicable in regards to provenance or style. They make up their own rules about marks and designers to sell more jewelry. Or in some cases, they see what they want to see to make their jewelry more valuable, whether it's misidentifying a stone type or misattributing a designer or mark. Whether errors are repeated innocently, or out and out deception is evident, the old "buyer beware" caution stands true here.

Don't get the idea that a few bad apples have to spoil the fun for everyone. Shoppers who want to make sure they're not getting taken when purchasing collectible jewelry will find this reference guide to be quite valuable as many of the not-so-good "tricks of the trade" are pointed out to help secondary market consumers make wise buying decisions. And most collectors will tell you they run across far more people who are trying to market jewelry ethically than crooked individuals who might take advantage of them. Those good folks are willing to remedy any mistakes they might make as they're helping collectors pursue their hobby. Even so, there's nothing like good old-fashioned knowledge when it comes to being an educated consumer, and that's the real basis for sharing all this information with you.

The Fun of Collecting

Don't think jewelry collecting is just about studying, though. That's part of it, certainly, and it can be a really enjoyable part of the hobby if you're into that sort of thing. If not, you can just buy what you like, wear it, and garner lots of compliments from others who notice your sparkle.

You can also enjoy keeping up with trends by participating in jewelry groups online, making friends attending conventions for jewelry collectors, watching what celebrities are wearing, and "pinning" all the latest vintage trends and sharing them through other types of social media. For instance, even if a modern bride opts for fresh flowers in her wedding bouquet, she's probably going to at least consider one made using vintage brooches pinned to oodles of ribbon beforehand. This clever use of vintage brooches has gotten a lot of attention lately.

It's also exciting for collectors to watch trends develop for things with interesting names such as saphiret jewelry and "dragon's breath" stones, both of which you'll learn about in Section Three of this guide. There are shifts in terminology to watch in describing contemporary jewelry such as "resin" to

Jomaz brooch set, c. 1950s, flawed emerald glass stones with rhinestone accents in rhodium-plated bow motif settings, marked Jomaz, brooch 1 3/4", earrings 1 1/2". **$325-$400**

Jewelry courtesy LinsyJsJewels.com

denote plastic components, which is actually the same term many companies used in the 1930s-1950s. And by participating online, collectors also find out about new names for unsigned jewelry to watch for, like the immensely popular Egyptian revival pieces made by Neiger in the first quarter of the 20th century. There's even a Facebook page you can "like" devoted to this topic.

And then there's the shopping. The thrill of the hunt and the next treasure you'll discover, well, that's what keeps all jewelry aficionados and collectors in general rocking along with their hobby. You'll make friends along the way as well, and that's perhaps the most fun of all. There's nothing like spending time with like-minded individuals to ooh and ahh over your latest finds.

To learn more about Costume Jewelry Collectors International, an organization co-founded by Melinda Lewis and me and dedicated to costume jewelry education and bringing collectors together to enjoy their hobby, visit www.cjci.co.

Regarding the Pricing in This Guide

You'll note this guide includes a broad spectrum of examples, from inexpensive figural pins to four-figure designer rarities. These pieces were chosen to give all readers, from those who are just trying to identify a variety of pieces they've inherited to avid collectors, the values for items they may own or aspire to own while educating them about the origin and age.

Even though the Internet has brought an equalizing factor to the table, values for collectible costume jewelry vary widely across the country and around the globe. For instance, in larger cities and tourist areas, shops carrying these goods tend to command higher prices. Internet sites catering to a high-end clientele may command higher prices than online auctions, and so on.

Rarity, designer/manufacturer attribution, quality, craftsmanship, and past selling history are all taken into consideration when determining estimates of value. Keep in mind the prices denoted in this reference are simply a guideline to follow based on the estimated values provided by the owners of the items depicted, including the author.

– *Pamela Y. Wiggins*

Section One
COSTUME JEWELRY THROUGH THE DECADES

One of the most interesting aspects of jewelry collecting is the influence of popular culture, historical events, and fashion on adornment worn during various periods. Celebrities, royalty, and the fashionable set have all had an impact on jewelry and how it has been worn throughout the decades. Jewelry was mentioned in fictional works penned early on, illustrated in magazines as soon as mass printing was feasible, and then photographed on the rich and famous even before designers became celebrities in the era of Coco Chanel and Elsa Schiaparelli's rivalry. What was in vogue from a fashion perspective also heavily influenced the jewelry styles of the day, especially with Queen Victoria's sway in the 1800s, and later on runways in Paris, New York, and Milan.

One thing to remember when dating jewelry by period is that styles were fluid. That is, Victorian-style jewelry most often found by collectors didn't stop being produced the moment Queen Victoria died in 1901, nor did late-Victorian jewelry have the same styling as earlier Victorian pieces. Bold 1950s rhinestones didn't go out of style the moment the clock ticked over to 1960, and so on. You'll often find an overlapping of periods, which means transitional pieces with a number of influences were made and worn during those timeframes. For example, you might find a piece that includes elements of Edwardian design but offers a taste of Art Deco flair as well. You'll also notice that prolific companies like Napier produced fashion forward styles in the early 1970s using components similar to designs they made in the 1950s.

And don't forget about those all-important revival pieces that have been made throughout jewelry history. Egyptian revivals occurred not only in the 1920s when King Tut's tomb was opened, but also prior to that time in the Victorian era and also in the 1970s when the Boy King's treasures were on tour once again. Victorian revivals have been around longer than the Queen's lengthy reign, and there have been many interpretations through the decades. Recently, bold rhinestones and showy gold-tone pieces have become popular again with the advent of the "statement" necklace, and some of those pieces also revive styles of the past. Those are just a few examples of how designers have been inspired by the looks of yesterday when creating fashion jewelry. Looking at construction and components used, as noted in Section Three, will provide clues about the age of a piece beyond examining the overall style and learning about the historical context of vintage pieces.

Lastly, these sections are appetizers, if you will, designed to whet your palate for more depending on what you hone in on as your favorites. Entire books could be written on each one of these sections, and in some cases have been. Go forth and research, as you find your interest piqued.

LATE VICTORIAN

1880-1900

Overall, the early-, mid-, and late-Victorian periods can be encapsulated into an era of sentiment. While clothing styles and the accompanying adornments decidedly changed during Queen Victoria's long reign in England, the jewelry produced from 1837-1901 was worn symbolically as much as it was worn to be fashionable.

Much of the antique costume jewelry found today that can truly be termed Victorian – those pieces dating to 1901 and earlier – is from the late-Victorian period beginning in 1880. The collector's focus tends to land in that area today because these items are found more often now in comparison to the older pieces, and most of the items illustrated in this guide are indeed late-Victorian. But one of the most interesting aspects of jewelry from this time frame carried over from the early- and mid-Victorian periods – 1837-1860 and 1861-1879, respectively – is the symbolism held in the designs.

Everything from a simple floral motif, such as a daisy signifying innocence, to the materials used in construction stood for something, whether it was the incorporation of coral to ward off evil spirits or the use of black components, and there are a number of them, to signify mourning. Examining these elements, along with the numerous influences Queen Victoria's choice of attire had on

Scarab pin, c. late 1800s, brass with molded art glass body set into scarab with tabs acting as prongs, 1 1/4" long.
$75-$95

Jewelry courtesy Brigitte Gervais

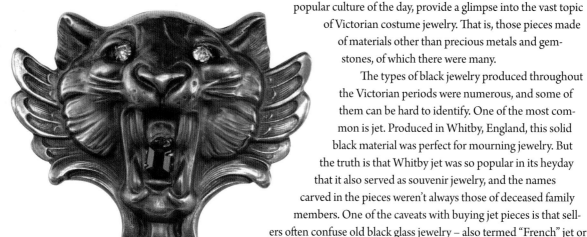

popular culture of the day, provide a glimpse into the vast topic of Victorian costume jewelry. That is, those pieces made of materials other than precious metals and gemstones, of which there were many.

The types of black jewelry produced throughout the Victorian periods were numerous, and some of them can be hard to identify. One of the most common is jet. Produced in Whitby, England, this solid black material was perfect for mourning jewelry. But the truth is that Whitby jet was so popular in its heyday that it also served as souvenir jewelry, and the names carved in the pieces weren't always those of deceased family members. One of the caveats with buying jet pieces is that sellers often confuse old black glass jewelry – also termed "French" jet or Vauxhall glass – with true jet, which is a natural substance. Some glass beads from the late 1800s were, in fact, cut with irregular facets to resemble jet. These are old and certainly collectible, but not as desirable as true jet to a fan of Victorian jewelry.

Tiger brooch, c. 1890s, molded brass with solid back (not a stamping) with clear rhinestones for eyes and red stone for mouth; later Joseff of Hollywood pieces were made in this style using Victorian inspired stampings, fastens with "C" clasp, unmarked, 2 5/8" wide. **$200-$250**

Author's Collection

The easiest way to determine if a piece is jet, and least likely to cause damage, is by judging the weight. A string of jet beads will weigh far less than a string of glass beads. Jet is so light in weight that it sometimes resembles plastic. Some people will tap a bead or component on their teeth to determine the material, since glass has a distinctive feel and sound about it. Or they hold the material to their cheek to see if it has a coolness associated with glass. Jet will feel warmer to the touch. And, if you rub an inconspicuous area of a piece of jet jewelry on a rough surface like cement or the bottom of a pottery vase, it will leave a brownish mark.

By the 1880s, although mourning jewelry was still present, styles and tastes began to change. Both men and women donned fancy cufflinks during this era. Smaller pins, including stickpins, featured a variety of themes and were also worn by both genders. Some of these reflected the increasing number of women interested in sporting pursuits with hunting dogs, horses, and game birds decorating them in ladies' styles. Even the ubiquitous cameos so prolific during the entire era were smaller when compared to early- to mid-Victorian adornment. Small pins sometimes had specific uses, such as holding clothing or lingerie in place.

Porcelain painting was a popular pastime for the Victorian lady as well. In addition to household items, this hand-painting practice extended to white "blanks" in oval or round shapes that were then mounted into brass frames with pin backs in a variety of sizes. These are still readily found today featuring colorful floral designs and other themes. Jewelry became more colorful in general in the late 1800s, in fact, with many more colored stones and enameling techniques coming about with Art Nouveau influence.

As manufacturing techniques continued to be refined, many jewelry items were made of metal stampings featuring a variety of motifs ranging from snakes, flowers, frogs, birds, and wild animals to beautiful women. Celluloid was also used as a substitute for tortoiseshell in hair combs during this period, but plastics in general weren't popular in mainstream jewelry-making until the 1920s.

Until the 1890s, earrings were of the pierced variety. The practice was then deemed "barbaric" and the first ear screws were patented in 1894. Looking at

1897 commemorative pin, c. 1897, silver-plated brooch from 1897, worn to commemorate the 60th year of Queen Victoria's reign, fastens with "C" clasp, unmarked, 1 1/4" wide. **$55-$75**

Jewelry courtesy ChicAntiques.com

Water lily brooch, c. 1890, stamped metal in an Art Nouveau design with a water lily as the focal point, fastens with "C" clasp, unmarked, 4" wide. **$50-$75**

Jewelry courtesy ChicAntiques.com

Water lily back view showing Victorian stamping detail and "C" clasp.

overall styles and components used in earrings from the Victorian era is paramount in dating them to the correct period, especially to avoid confusing them with later "revival" styles that came into fashion decades later.

Both fringe necklaces and festoons, with draping swags of chain, glass beads or simulated pearls, were popular in costume jewelry made during the latter part of the 1800s. Lavalieres with Art Nouveau motifs were quite fashionable during the 1890s as well. And as the end of the century approached, the bayadère, made by twisting two strands of beads or pearls together, came into fashion along with the dog collar popularized by then Princess Alexandra.

Cut steel buckle, c. late 1800s, two-part buckle made of cut steel "stones" riveted to steel backing, 2 1/2" wide. **$50-$75**

Jewelry courtesy ChicAntiques.com

Porcelain pin, c. late 1890s, porcelain set in brass backing with transfer print of woman, hand-applied gold paint and simulated turquoise jewels, fastens with "C" clasp, 1 1/4" diameter. **$95-$125**

Jewelry courtesy ChicAntiques.com

Sash pin, c. 1890, black glass and enameled metal frame made to simulate jet, fastens with "C" clasp, unmarked, 3" wide. **$55-$75**

Jewelry courtesy ChicAntiques.com

Blue stomacher, c. late 1800s, heavy brass construction with tiny eyes to be sewn on garment, prong set in a geometric pattern with white, royal blue, and dark blue pastes, 6" wide. **$350-$450**

Jewelry courtesy Brigitte Gervais

Pierced earrings in original box, c. 1890s, petite earrings made of brass stampings with rhinestone dangles, in original crushed velvet box, pierced with screw posts, earrings measure just over 1 1/4" long. **$50-$75**

Jewelry courtesy ChicAntiques.com

Owl pin, c. late 1800s, brass with paste eyes, simple "C" clasp, likely English in origin, 3 3/8" long. **$250-$300**

Jewelry courtesy Brigitte Gervais

Tiny cameo, c. 1890s, shell carving of a Victorian woman's silhouette under a tree set in brass, possibly a depiction of Rebecca at the well, just over 3/4" long. **$65-$95**

Jewelry courtesy ChicAntiques.com

Moon man pin, c. late 1800s, heavy gold plate on brass with high domed faceted paste set into star, man in moon is pale blue molded glass with mirror backing, fastens with "C" clasp, 1 3/8" diameter. **$300-$400**

Jewelry courtesy Brigitte Gervais

Victorian Sash Pins

One of the most commonly found styles of brooch from the late-Victorian era is the sash pin, used to fasten an over-the-shoulder sash at the waist, adding a bit of color to even the most staid mourning dress. It should come as no surprise that this fashion statement originated with Queen Victoria and was widely embraced by the masses.

These brooches are usually fairly large in comparison to other styles made in the late 1800s, and they have a very thick pin stem that fastens with a "C"-style clasp (see Section Three for an example of this type of clasp). Many have definitive Art Nouveau characteristics such as sinuous lines; elements taken from nature – birds, flowers, leaves, vines; or other decorative curling elements popular at that time. Most have sparse embellishment in terms of stones, although some do sport enameling or other decorative features. The more elaborate examples with unusual design elements garner the highest prices. Sash pins can stand alone as an interesting collection, and many can still be purchased quite reasonably in comparison to other types of jewelry from this era.

Sash pin, c. 1890s, highly stylized dolphins flank each side of a high domed bezel-set art glass cabochon, background is ornately done with feather-like swirls stamped into the metal, fastens with "C" clasp, 3 1/2" wide. $250-$350

Jewelry courtesy Brigitte Gervais

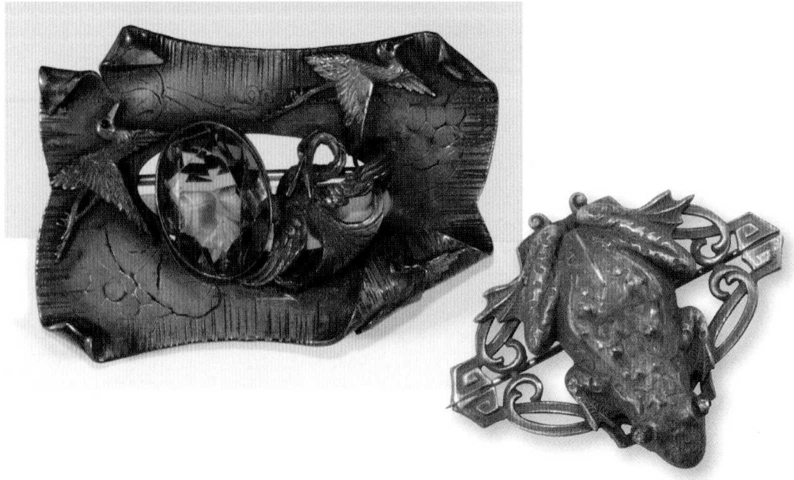

Art Nouveau birds sash pin, c. 1890s, large glass oval unfoiled stone set in heavy brass surrounded by applied birds with tiny green glass cabochon knife-set eyes, fastens with "C" clasp, 2 7/8" wide. $250-$300

Author's Collection

FAR RIGHT **Single frog sash pin, c. 1890s, patinated bronze-colored metal with glass cabochon jewel, fastens with "C" clasp, 2 3/8" wide. $250-$300**

Jewelry courtesy Brigitte Gervais

EDWARDIAN

1900-1920

If you're a fan of the PBS television series "Downton Abbey," you've seen many transitional pieces combining Victorian elements with more modern styles worn by the ladies on the program, which begins in 1912 with the sinking of the Titanic.

The years leading up to that time were transitional in terms of jewelry manufacture, with Victorian influences still very much in play and the trends started by Edward and Alexandra, even before they became king and queen in 1901, still alive and well. In fact, some jewelry historians see the Edwardian era extending from 1890 through 1920.

For the purposes of classifying costume jewelry and circa dating, however, it's often easier to look at what was going on in jewelry design in the first two decades of the 20th century. There were actually a number of influences in design including Victorian, Arts & Crafts, Art Nouveau, and Edwardian styles, and some of them were commingled a bit. Later during this period, some Victorian influences remained, but touches of Art Deco elements were certainly evident.

In other words, many of the jewelry styles from the 1900 to 1920 period aren't nearly as distinct as the Victorian mourning jewelry that came before, or the Art Deco geometrics that came after. Society was in flux and moving toward the modern with the advent of automobiles, electricity, telephones, and airplanes, and this change from old to new was reflected in the adornment of the period as well.

However, pieces made closer to 1900 do tend to have Victorian influences akin to the "Gibson Girl" silhouette, while pieces made in the timeframe around World War I can most certainly include a nod toward Art Deco elements found even more readily in the 1920s and 1930s. For this reason, many pieces of Edwardian jewelry are sometimes inadvertently misidentified as older or newer by both sellers and collectors.

One thing that many pieces made early in the early 1900s have in common is filigree work, and this in some minds solidly represents the term Edwardian. Costume jewelry in this style was done in sterling silver or base metal with white metal finishes imitating platinum with decidedly lacy elements. These may contain semi-precious gemstones or they may be embellished with unfoiled glass or paste stones to mimic fine jewelry.

Garland-style influences with swags of leaves, florets, bows, and tassels were also an Edwardian staple, and these motifs were interpreted in both fine and costume jewelry of the day. These looks represented the old guard with an emphasis on the materials being used rather than innovative design.

Arts & Crafts ideals and Art Nouveau elements carried over from the 1800s ushered in the new looks embraced early in the century. The emphasis

Pearl earrings, c. 1910-1920, pot metal with nickel plating, screw backs, glass button pearls and pastes set into pear-shaped drop, 3" long. **$125-$150**

Jewelry courtesy Brigitte Gervais

Gold-filled filigree brooch, c. 1915-1920, square glass aquamarines, combines Edwardian-style filigree with Art Deco-influenced geometric stones, closes with safety clasp, 2" long. **$55-$75**

Jewelry courtesy ChicAntiques.com

RIGHT E.A. Bliss brooch, c. 1910, filigree silver-tone metal with old style flat-back rhinestones and small jewel and colored bead accents in blue, green, clear, purple, and amber, closes with "C" clasp, marked E.A. Co. for E.A. Bliss, the forerunner to Napier, 2 7/8" x 2 1/2". **$150-$200**

Jewelry courtesy ChicAntiques.com

FAR RIGHT Dangle pearl earrings, c. 1900-1910, silver plate on brass screw backs, wax-filled hollow glass beads strung on wire with cut steel seed beads, central plaque has ornate framing with five filigree chain drops terminating with a drop pearl, 3 1/2" long. **$150-$175**

Jewelry courtesy Brigitte Gervais

was on imagination, fantasy, interpretive design, and quality craftsmanship. Jewelry of this nature usually incorporated vividly colored stones and bright enameling. The expressive nature of these styles – with flowing lines in the form of vines and tendrils, bold leaves, lilies, dragonflies, bats, and other natural motifs – is often distinctive and easily identifiable, although dating is a bit more precarious because of the Victorian overlap. In most cases it's easier to label these pieces as circa 1900 and call it a day, keeping in mind that many of these styles have been reproduced, and looking for signs of age and appropriate components when dating is vital.

Necklaces took on some new looks in the early 1900s. The first version of the sautoir was a wide, long necklace made of beads or faux pearls terminating in a tassel or pendant. Other necklace styles of the period included the negligee pendant, which incorporated a pair of drops dangling from fine chain in unequal lengths. Both of these styles transitioned from fine jewelry to costume jewelry in Edwardian and Art Nouveau variations. The lavaliere continued to be popular during this era as well, and many were made with metal filigree components. Choker necklaces were also worn during this period.

Smallish pins remained in vogue during this period, including filigree bar pins with stones imitating fine jewelry, although they could sometimes be rather long. During the World War I era, around 1915 or so, safety catches came into use on costume jewelry designs. Prior to this time, they were mostly used in fine jewelry manufacture.

Earrings were, by and large, screw backs with more and more made in this style rather than pierced approaching the 1920s. Large and lavishly embellished shoe buckles adorned footwear made during this period as well.

Heart mirror pendant, c. 1900-1910, enameled heart portrait pendant with Art Nouveau styling along the edges, slides open to reveal a mirror, marked 900 for coin silver, 2 1/2" long. **$195-$295**

Jewelry courtesy ChicAntiques.com

Bird articulated sew on, c. 1910-1920, base metal with white metal plating, wings are articulated and attached to shoulders by a simple hook, set with tiny pavé set pastes, meant to be sewn onto a garment via circular attachments, 8 1/2" wide. **$200-$250**

Jewelry courtesy Brigitte Gervais

Filigree brooch, c. 1910, white metal-plated filigree with simulated diamond in center, closes with an early safety clasp, 1 7/8" long and 7/8" wide. **$65-$85**

Jewelry courtesy ChicAntiques.com

Ruby bar pin, c. 1900-1910, silver-tone metal with Art Nouveau influence, simulated ruby center stone with invisibly set simulated rubies on either side, closes with "C" clasp, 2 3/8" wide. **$45-$65**

Jewelry courtesy ChicAntiques.com

GEMSCOPE
an in-depth look

Ostby & Barton Titanic Connection

This Providence, Rhode Island company, established in the late 1870s by Engelhart Cornelius Østby and Nathan B. Barton, was widely known for producing quality rings and other karat gold jewelry. Costume pieces like the circa-1910 sterling bangle bracelet shown here are also occasionally found. Jewelry made by Ostby & Barton is marked "OB" with Sterling, 10K or 14K, if applicable. What draws many collectors to these pieces today, however, is Østby's connection to the infamous Titanic ocean liner. Although early reports in Providence indicated that he and his daughter, Helen, were safe, only the girl survived. Apparently Østby went back to his first class cabin to retrieve warmer clothing as the ship began to sink, and his daughter was whisked away on a lifeboat while he was gone. Østby went down with the ship, and the girl never saw her father again, according to Encyclopedia-Titanica.org. While the jewelry made by Ostby & Barton has a marginal connection to the Titanic at best, the mystique of that unfortunate voyage adds intrigue to the jewelry.

Floral filigree brooch, c. 1915-1920, gold-plated base metal with emerald green glass stones and clear accents (clear stones are likely vintage replacements), old style safety clasp, 3" wide. **$65-$95**

Jewelry courtesy ChicAntiques.com

Filigree necklace set, c. 1910-1920, white metal filigree with sapphire blue glass stones and clear accents, old style spring ring clasps, necklace 18" long, bracelet 7" long. **$275-$350**

Jewelry courtesy LinsyJsJewels.com

Garland rhinestone earrings, c. 1910, pot metal with white metal plating and knife set pastes, screw backs, oval garland drop has articulated smaller oval center, 2 3/4" long. **$150-$175**

Jewelry courtesy Brigitte Gervais

Diamonbar sterling bracelet, c. 1917, transitional piece with both Edwardian and Art Deco influences made of sterling silver with clear and blue rhinestones, buckle-style clasp patented in 1917, bracelet 7" long. **$125-$175**

Jewelry courtesy ChicAntiques.com

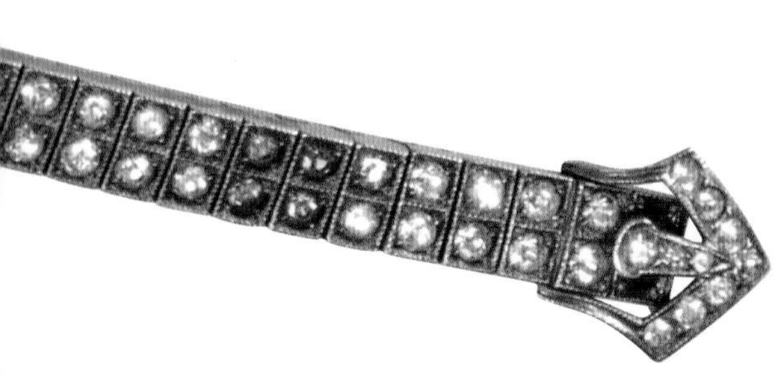

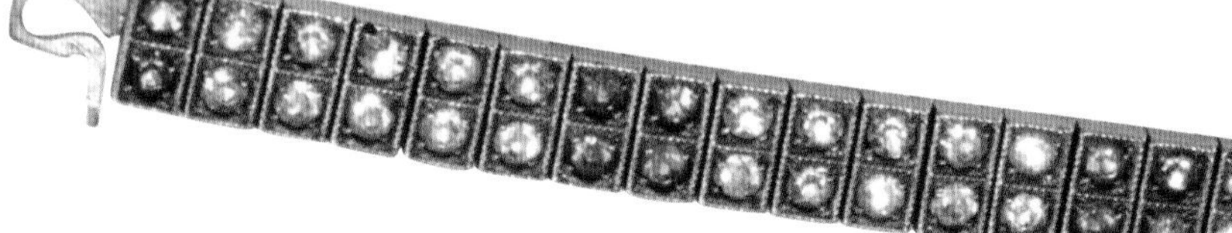

1920s

COSTUME JEWELRY THROUGH THE DECADES

Most people think Art Deco when they think 1920s. But it was also the decade of the emerging designer when Coco Chanel and Elsa Schiaparelli firmly cemented their stakes as Parisian trendsetters. Unlike the costume jewelry made in prior decades, with the exception of Arts & Crafts and Art Nouveau pieces, a greater emphasis was put on design over material. It became more important than ever to complement the wardrobe with accessories if one wanted to remain fashionable. Nevertheless, designer names weren't quite "there" yet, and most jewelry was sold unbranded during this decade.

Emerging trends included jewelry made in sterling silver with marcasites, rock crystal, onyx, carnelian, lapis, coral, and jade. German pieces with the Theodor Fahrner "TF" mark are some of the most popular examples of this type of jewelry. Lesser jewelry copied this look in silver-plated base metal with imitations of semi-precious stones, and these are found more often now than the work of Fahrner's company.

By the late 1920s, revivals of Victorian and Edwardian era designs were already becoming fashionable. For instance, the Napier mark wasn't used until 1922, but a number of the company's early marked pieces have a decidedly lacy look about them akin to Victorian or Edwardian styles (see Napier in Section Two for more examples). This jewelry was distinguished by updated materials and construction techniques, such as chunkier filigree and gold-tone metalwork, when compared to pieces truly dating from 1890-1910.

Many Victorian revival styles made in Czechoslovakia were introduced during the 1920s as well, and these remained popular into the 1930s. Some are marked simply "Czech," and rather obscurely, so all components must be examined carefully, even the insides of jump ring closures. Many of these styles are made of stamped gold-plated metal filigree and set with stones in bright primary hues. Some pieces incorporated enameled leaves as well. Geometrically cut or molded stones also imparted an Art Deco feel to some jewelry from this region, and pieces with Asian motifs were made using jade-colored glass. Many glass-beaded sautoirs were also made using Czech components.

Celluloid became a more popular medium for jewelry crafting during this era. Many pieces were made to simulate ivory (sometimes referred to as "French ivory" by marketers to artificially elevate its status) and to imitate coral and tortoiseshell. Rhinestone-embellished bangle bracelets from this decade are a favorite among plastics enthusiasts. These range in size from

Knoll & Pregizer Art Deco sterling "emerald and diamond" paste bracelet, c. 1925, bracelet made in Germany using sterling silver with clear and emerald-colored paste in fine jewelry style; each link is curved to fit the wrist and is fully articulated, fastens with a figure-eight safety clasp, marked on the reverse 935 (the European mark for high grade sterling) and the trademark stamp of intersecting letters KP within a lily; shown with its original jewelry store leather and velvet fitted case from a store in Buenos Aires where it was purchased by its original owner. **$3,500-$4,500**

Jewelry courtesy Robin Deutsch Collection

narrow spacers to multi-rows of rhinestones, and the most desirable have painted accents in Art Deco designs. Collectors have learned that celluloid can rapidly decompose when it becomes "diseased" from improper storage in cold or hot areas, or when exposed to extreme moisture. Exposure to corroding metal can also cause this problem. Pieces with cracks, crazing or other signs of deterioration should be discarded as this condition is contagious and can spread to other jewelry stored in proximity.

Some early plastics, especially colorful examples, are misidentified as celluloid, but they are actually made of cellulose acetate. When warmed with hot water, celluloid smells of camphor, while cellulose acetate emits an odor similar to vinegar. Take care when wetting pieces that are embellished with stones. Water may loosen the glue holding the stones in place, causing them to fall out, and it's often hard to find exact replacements for restoration with older stones. Painted designs on these pieces should also be protected from water damage.

The sautoir of the Edwardian period morphed into extremely long flapper-style strands of beads or pearls. Long necklaces were worn draped down the back as well. Other popular 1920s necklace styles include lariat styles in both long beaded varieties and shorter versions with briolette drops on delicate chains. The "Y" necklace was introduced during this period as well, and it was extremely popular in styles ranging from copies of fine jewelry to beads. The choker necklace also remained fashionable.

Screw back earrings were the norm during this era, and dangle styles were all the rage. Many with Art Deco geometric designs were made with clear rhinestones, and some sported contrasting colors of black or green in both genuine onyx and jade or with simulated glass pieces or marcasite accents. Rhinestone and beaded headbands in varying sizes became extremely popular during this era, some of which covered most of the forehead when worn. Others had elaborate side embellishments.

Some brooches typical of the era featured Art Deco geometrics. Other jewelry depicted airplanes, fancy cars, gazelles, or women with sleek dogs denoting wealth and/or speed, both idyllic symbols of the Roaring '20s.

Jade glass necklace, c. 1920s, jade green melon-shaped beads with stamped silver-tone metal links and pendant comprised of layered stampings, unmarked, 16" long. **$400-$550**

Jewelry courtesy LinsyJsJewels.com

Gold filigree bracelet, c. late 1920s, emerald green glass stone set in gold-plated filigree metal with clear rhinestone accents, 7/8" wide. **$125-$150**

Jewelry courtesy LinsyJsJewels.com

Hinged cuff bracelet, c. 1920s, Edwardian filigree carried over from the World War I era combined with a hint of Art Deco symmetry, silver-tone metal with gold-tone accents and emerald-cut topaz rhinestone, unmarked, just under 1" at the widest point. **$75-$100**

Jewelry courtesy ChicAntiques.com

Czech brooch, c. late 1920s, emerald green and ruby red glass stones with white enamel set in gold-plated filigree metal, marked Czechoslovakia, 3" wide. **$240-$285**

Jewelry courtesy LinsyJsJewels.com

Czech glass necklace, c. late 1920s, red molded glass stones set in brass pronged findings, 16" long. **$225-$265**

Jewelry courtesy LinsyJsJewels.com

Art Deco bracelet, c. late 1920s-early 1930s, pot metal setting with round and baguette rhinestones in geometric design, unmarked, 7" long x 1" wide. **$125-$150**

Author's Collection

Napier filigree necklace, c. late 1920s, filigree stampings with faceted blue glass beads, each link is two stampings back to back so the necklace is reversible with no clasp, slips over head, marked Napier, 29" long with 3 1/2" pendant. **$250-$325**

Author's Collection

Necklace, c. 1920s, emerald green glass beads with large diamond-shaped unfoiled center stone, unmarked, 18" long.
$125-$200

Jewelry courtesy LinsyJsJewels.com

GEMSCOPE
an in-depth look

Fishel Nessler Art Deco Bracelet

This articulated sterling silver bracelet, c. 1925, is set with 16 alternating links filled with French-cut baguettes, each accented with a single round bead set paste on either side within a triangular-shaped setting. The mark as shown on the back of the clasp is a fish symbol containing the word "sterling" on the body with an "L" in its mouth for Fishel Nessler, an American company based in New York City. This family-owned business, with a rocky history including a suicide attempt and bankruptcy, was in business in different iterations from 1886 to 1937. This substantial bracelet weighs 35.7 grams and measures 6 1/2" long x 1/2" at the widest link. **Est. $475-$675**

Jewelry courtesy Robin Deutsch Collection

A Note Related to the Fishel Nessler Brand: *There has been an unsubstantiated rumor circulating on the Internet for several years that Carl M. Fishel of Trifari, Krussman & Fishel left Fishel Nessler to join Trifari. Avid Trifari collector and jewelry historian Robin Deutsch has found this assessment to be untrue, as Carl Fishel was never documented as an associate of Fishel Nessler in any capacity. Carl Fishel worked for Rice & Hochster, a company specializing in hair ornaments and shoe buckles. According to historical records, including his obituary, Fishel's employment with Rice & Hochster has been confirmed as 1900 through 1925. He then left to join his ex-associates from Rice & Hochster (who had already formed Trifari & Krussman by that time), to establish a new firm: Trifari, Krussman & Fishel. Carl M. Fishel was president of Trifari and died in 1964. Fishel Nessler jewelry should be appreciated and collected on its own merit as quality costume jewelry without false attributions associating it with Trifari.*

Tortoise glass necklace, c. late 1920s-early 1930s, glass stones colored to imitate tortoiseshell alternating with embossed findings made of white metal, unmarked, 16 1/2" long. **$185-$235**

Jewelry courtesy LinsyJsJewels.com

Art Deco Bakelite bracelet, c. late 1920s, six rectangular emerald green Bakelite links alternate with triple row of pierced rhinestone connector links of bead-set rhinestones set in millegrain-edged chromium-plated base metal, 7 1/2" long x 3/4" wide. **$350-$550**

Jewelry courtesy the Robin Deutsch Collection

1930s

COSTUME JEWELRY THROUGH THE DECADES

The 1930s saw the dawning of the true designer brand in costume jewelry history. Chanel and Schiaparelli set the stage earlier, but things didn't really get rolling until the fine jewelry economy fell apart during the Great Depression and a wide market opened up for enterprising costume jewelers. It was a decade where fine jewelry was copied shamelessly as "junk jewelry."

Ciner moved from producing fine jewelry to making sterling pieces embellished with rhinestones. Trifari, Kushman and Fishel employed Alfred Philippe, who brought with him magnificent ideas gleaned from his work in the fine jewelry industry, and Marcel Boucher's early MB (sometimes referenced as a "bird" although it's actually a French Phrygian cap atop the initials MB) marked pieces reflect his time spent working as a jeweler and model maker for Cartier. Coro also patented its first Art Deco Duettes in 1931 (learn more about Coro's Duette in Section Two) based on fine jewelry that came before.

Those early Duette brooch mechanisms held small-hinged clips. Clips like these were produced widely by a variety of companies and came in all shapes and sizes. The smaller versions were most often sold in pairs; larger dress clips were usually sold singly rather than two at a time. Some of the most intriguing dress clips are those made in the late 1930s by Eisenberg, a brand known for marketing jewelry using high quality stones set in heavy cast designs.

Companies like these saw the costume jewelry industry as big business. They employed teams of designers, model makers, stone setters and other skilled craftspeople, and many of these talented folks had left the fine jewelry industry looking for work as their jobs were eliminated in the throes of the Depression.

Dime stores were frequented more than ever during this era. Ladies sought inexpensive trinkets there to bring a little joy into their lives without spending a small fortune. Bakelite jewelry can be counted among those numerous colorful treasures with bangle bracelets, whimsical pins, and beautifully carved dress clips leading the way.

There were actually a number of other trademarked phenolic plastics used for jewelry manufacture, including Prystal and Catalin. In fact, colorless Bakelite was termed Prystal in 1935. The term Bakelite is frequently used as a generic term for all these pieces now, although the Catalin Corp. purportedly made more jewelry than other brands. Prices have cooled among collectors as more and more copies of great pieces, also known as "Fakelite," have flooded the market. Nevertheless, this early plastic still has a good following and it makes an impressive and fun collection to display. (Learn more about identifying Bakelite in Section Three of this guide.)

Also introduced by DuPont in 1937 was Lucite, a trade name for its version of acrylic resin. Jewelry production quickly began using this new type of plastic in both clear and tinted hues, which continued into the 1940s and 1950s.

Americans also turned to the movies to escape the doldrums of everyday life, and both men and women frequently copied the styles worn by Hollywood

Pot metal vacationer pin, c. 1930s, enameled palm tree with woman carrying rhinestone luggage, unmarked, 2 1/2" long. **$55-$75**

Author's Collection

Filigree faux amethyst, pearl, and enamel hinged Art Deco bangle bracelet, c.1930, intricately pierced filigree decorated with a faceted unfoiled glass amethyst stone surrounded by tiny pearls and bordered with enamel, chromium-plated base metal, rectangular central element 1 1/2" x 1". **$850-$950**

Jewelry courtesy Robin Deutsch Collection

stars. More revival jewelry was made, including Victorian revivals inspired by the Civil War epic "Gone with the Wind," using updated construction techniques and components. Joseff of Hollywood supplied much of the costume jewelry to the film industry in period-appropriate styles with special Russian gold plating that worked well under studio lighting. The late 1930s also saw Joseff introduce a retail line of jewelry sold in select stores across the country.

Filigree work was indeed still used for some jewelry made in the 1930s, especially early in the decade. The filigree hinged bangle example with a large central simulated amethyst featured above is an exceptional piece given the additions of enameling and faux pearl accents, which are rarely seen in this type of bracelet. The width of this bracelet also makes it unique at just over 1" wide. It's interesting to note that bracelets in general became a bit wider in this decade, even when made in styles carried over from the 1920s.

Many pieces of pot metal jewelry were made during the Depression years, including the aforementioned dress clips, and many were done in Art Deco styles in the early 1930s. Pot metal, quite simply, is unplated base metal that has a dull gray finish. The pieces can be plain with rhinestone embellishments or be enameled. Higher quality jewelry employed plating over base metal, which can be gold- or silver-tone in color. Rhodium was not commonly used to impart a platinum look in jewelry until the early 1930s. Chrome or nickel was used previously, and the finish is not as fine as that found on rhodium-plated pieces. Companies like Mazer, Trifari, and Boucher used high quality rhodium plating during this period.

Monogram jewelry, most often featuring one to three initials, surged in popularity in the 1930s as well. Companies like Monocraft, the forerunner to Monet, created designs that could be tailored to a customer's preference right in the store – no special order necessary. Their "Click Its" and "Dangles" lines were attached to silver- and gold-tone frames to complete pins, some with Art Deco influence, and these are the items collectors run across most often today. Necklaces and bracelets were also made, especially in the Dangles line, but these are a bit harder to find now. Other unknown manufacturers produced this type of personalized, customizable jewelry as well, and some date back to the 1920s moving into the 1930s with marcasite embellishments.

Overall, jewelry styles grew bolder as the 1930s progressed. By the end of the decade, retro styles with more curving lines were gaining popularity and becoming more prevalent in jewelry design as the demand for Art Deco styling cooled.

Pin, c. 1930s, enameled palm tree in gold-plated pot metal setting with dangling monkey and coconut, unmarked, 3" wide. **$75-$95**

Author's Collection

Art Deco faux ruby diamond paste sterling earrings, c. 1935, rhodium-plated sterling pendant earrings, each earring made in three sections to be fully articulated, screw back surmounts support a geometric pendant comprised of bead set pastes with a navette center highlighted with black enamel and finished with a large square cut ruby glass stone, 2 1/4" long x 1 1/4" wide, marked STERLING GERMANY. **$675-$875**

Jewelry courtesy Robin Deutsch Collection

Matched bangles, c. 1930s, red and yellow Bakelite with pineapple and leaf carving, unmarked, 3/4" wide. **$75-$95 each**

Author's Collection

Parrot pin, c. 1930s, pavé set rhinestones in pot metal setting with enameled beak and claws, unmarked, 3" long. $55-$75

Author's Collection

Dress clip, c. early 1930s, ornate clip with square, round, and baguette rhinestones set in pot metal with heavy gold plating, unmarked, 2 7/8" wide. **$125-$150**

Author's Collection

Bakelite, Lucite and celluloid set, c. 1930s, carved black Bakelite combined with clear Lucite and celluloid chain, unmarked, necklace 18", earrings 3/4", stretch bracelet. **$175-$225**

Jewelry courtesy ChicAntiques.com

Bangle, c. 1930s, butterscotch-colored Bakelite with rose carving, unmarked, just under 1" wide. **$135-$185**

Jewelry courtesy ChicAntiques.com

Monet Jewelers necklace, c. late 1930s, rare example of Monet rhinestone and enamel jewelry, Victorian Revival festoon-style with pink and blue rhinestones and quality navy blue and white enameling, marked with "Monet Jewelers" hangtag, filigree centerpiece, 3 3/4" long, overall length 16".
$550-$650

Jewelry courtesy ChicAntiques.com

Perfume pendant, c. 1930s, glass strawberry with flashed red coloring with bracc ccrow top, unmarked, 2" long.
$65-$95

Jewelry courtesy ChicAntiques.com

Necklace, c. 1930s, royal blue unfoiled rhinestones strung together in brass settings, unmarked, 16 1/2". **$150-$200**

Jewelry courtesy ChicAntiques.com

Compact pendant, c. 1930s, painted enamel compact pendant opens to reveal puff inside, unmarked, 1 3/4" diameter. **$85-$125**

Jewelry courtesy ChicAntiques.com

Embossed pendant necklace, c. 1930s, gold-plated pot metal setting with brilliant pink rhinestones, unmarked, chain 24" long, pendant 2 3/4" long. **$95-$135**

Jewelry courtesy ChicAntiques.com

Multicolor brooch, c. 1930s, likely of Czech origin based on style, stones, and construction; pink, blue, yellow, and purple rhinestones in varying hues and shapes, unmarked, 3 1/8" wide. **$85-$125**

Jewelry courtesy ChicAntiques.com

1940s

COSTUME JEWELRY THROUGH THE DECADES

Most people think of World War II when the 1940s come to mind, and this was definitely an influence on jewelry production during the early- to mid-1940s. In fact, Sweetheart Jewelry was prolific during this period. This type of jewelry was not only purchased and worn by those showing their patriotism on the home front, but in some cases it took the form of trench art sent home by soldiers to their sweethearts and other family members. Styles ranged from items showing a military affiliation to those worn by mothers signifying how many of their sons were in the service. These usually have stars representing each child. Pieces bearing three stars are hard to find, more than three stars is considered rare.

Much of the metal jewelry made after 1942, including many Sweetheart pieces, was produced in sterling silver when the war effort ramped up and rationing of base metals began. Sterling with a gold or rose gold "wash," which is a light form of plating, was substituted for jewelry made of pot metal seen in prior decades and even in the early 1940s.

Throughout the 1940s a style often referenced by collectors as "Retro," more formally Retro Modern, influenced jewelry design. Characteristics include curving metalwork, often made of sterling with a gold wash, and very few rhinestones or other embellishments.

Fewer rhinestones were used in pieces made during this time in general because it was nearly impossible to import them from Austria and Czechoslovakia. Pearls previously imported from Japan also ran short once jewelry-making supplies were depleted. Other materials came into use and virtually all American costume jewelry manufacturers adapted to find alternatives.

Miriam Haskell incorporated materials like wood, plastic, and seashells into her mid-1940s designs, all of which are unmarked but can be identified by the construction (see Section Three). Trifari used flawed slabs of acrylic resin, or Lucite, that weren't suitable for airplane windshields to craft its famous "jelly belly" jewelry (see "Jelly Belly" in Section Three for more on this type of "stone"). Coro, Boucher, and Eisenberg were known to have had at least some of their sterling jewelry produced in Mexico during this time as well. Joseff of Hollywood actually shifted its entire operation to manufacture airplane components during the war.

One thing some collectors don't realize, however, is that pieces of jewelry made of sterling were sometimes duplicated in base metals after the war by the same companies that originally made them. Coro's famous Rockfish brooch is one example. These are sometimes misidentified as reproductions, even though the older brooches are of the same quality as the sterling examples. Of course, the reason for this is that some pretty realistic-looking reproductions of this design were definitely made much later on, so it's always wise to proceed with caution in this area.

Plastics were widely used for jewelry manufacture during this decade rife with rationing, and a number of Bakelite figurals with patriotic themes were made.

Staret Lady Liberty brooch, c. 1940, finely enameled with red rhinestones and clear accents, 4" long. **$800-$1,000**

Jewelry courtesy LinsyJsJewels.com

Vogue sterling bracelet set, c. 1940s, large emerald green glass stones surrounded by green and clear accents, bracelet band comprised of bezel set green rhinestones, bracelet 6 3/4", brooch 2 1/8". **$400-$550**

Jewelry courtesy LinsyJsJewels.com

Acrylic resin and Bakelite were also combined with wood to produce fanciful figurals that are nothing short of fun to wear. After the war, Bakelite was too expensive to work with, and acrylic resin became a more popular medium for plastic jewelry. Occupied Japan figurals imported after the war were also made of celluloid.

Another type of plastic jewelry made in the late 1940s and into the 1950s is the acrylic resin and rhinestone "Forbidden Fruit." Fruit pins and earrings have actually been found on the original cards bearing this moniker and indicating their origin as Austria. The style, construction, and kitschy nature of these pieces are spot on for this timeframe in jewelry history. They usually incorporate some type of metalwork, such as a stem or leaves with light enameled accents. They aren't rare by any means, but they do have a following with collectors who look for unique styles and color combinations.

Duettes continued to be popular during this decade as well. Many of the examples made in the 1940s were beautifully enameled figurals made by Coro under the popular Corocraft brand. Some were sterling; others were made of base metal with silver or gold plating, depending on when they were manufactured during this tumultuous decade. (See "Coro" in Section Two for examples.)

Movies continued to play a major role in entertainment in the 1940s, and what the stars wore on film continued to influence popular fashion. Jewelry inspired by the movies was also made. Early in the decade licensed designs inspired by Alexander Korda's "Thief of Bagdad" and "The Jungle Book" were marketed. These were designed and produced by a company named Rice-Weiner, rather than Korda himself, in spite of the mark on the back of the pieces.

It's also interesting to note that Rice-Weiner made jewelry designed by McClelland Barclay from the mid-1930s through the early 1940s using the marks "McClelland Barclay" or occasionally "Barclay" (in the same Art Deco typeface as that found in the two-word mark). In 1946, a new company was founded, which signed its jewelry "Barclay" in script letters. McClelland Barclay perished in the war in 1943, so the script-marked pieces have no connection to this famed illustrator and designer, nor do they look like his Art Deco pieces. Norman Bel Geddes also designed a limited line for Rice-Weiner in 1949, launched in the summer of 1950, without much success.

The costume jewelry world lost another treasure in 1948 when Eugene Joseff, founder of Joseff of Hollywood, died when the plane he was piloting went down on the way to the family's ranch in Arizona. His wife, Joan Castle, who had worked in the business until the birth of their son, Jeffrey, in 1947, took over the operation, continuing her husband's legacy. Not only did she keep alive the tradition of renting period jewelry copies to the film industry, she kept the brand's retail lines in production into the prosperous 1950s.

Boucher sterling flower, c. mid-1940s, sapphire blue rhinestones with clear accents, sterling silver with gold wash, marked MB (old mark with Phrygian cap), 3 1/4" long. **$300-$400**

Jewelry courtesy LinsyJsJewels.com

RIGHT Heart tank brooch, c. early 1940s, red plastic heart with applied metal tank, plastic red, white, and blue dangles, 3 1/4" long. **$525-$700**

Jewelry courtesy LinsyJsJewels.com

FAR RIGHT Flag brooch, c. early 1940s, red and clear rhinestone stripes with blue "stars," flag portion 2 1/2" wide. **$125-$150**

Jewelry courtesy ChicAntiques.com

Remember Pearl Harbor sweetheart pin, c. early 1940s, central faux pearl surrounded by red, clear, and blue rhinestones with red and blue enameled lettering, gold plating over base metal, 3 1/2" wide. **$450-$600**

Jewelry courtesy LinsyJsJewels.com

Victory Torch brooch, c. early 1940s, red, clear, and blue rhinestones set in gold-plated metal, 2 1/8" long. **$150-$200**

Jewelry courtesy LinsyJsJewels.com

Caveat Turbator fur clip, c. early 1940s, red, clear, and blue rhinestones surround enameling, hornet's nest signifies World War II bomb squadron, 2 1/2" long. **$225-$325**

Jewelry courtesy LinsyJsJewels.com

Airplane pin, c. early 1940s, red, clear, and blue rhinestones set in cast pot metal with propellers and landing gear beneath, 2 7/8" long. **$100-$125**

Jewelry courtesy LinsyJsJewels.com

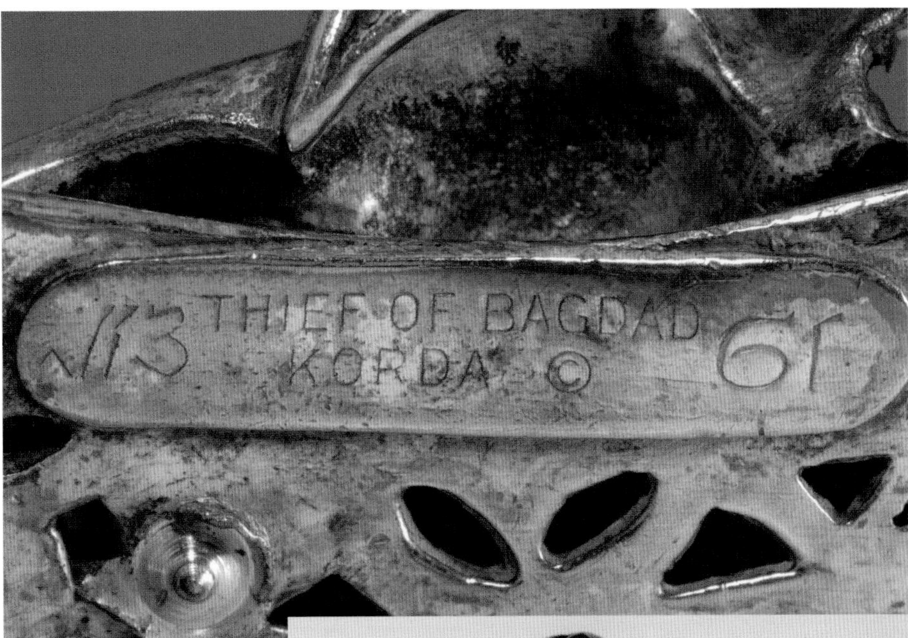

Korda flying carpet brooch, c. 1940, made in conjunction with the movie "Thief of Bagdad" by Alexander Korda; marked Thief of Bagdad Korda (although the piece was made by Rice-Weiner), 3" long. **$100-$150**

Jewelry courtesy OhioAntiques.com

Wooden brooch, c. 1940s, carved profile of an American Indian elder, unmarked, 3" tall. **$65-$95**

Jewelry courtesy ChicAntiques.com

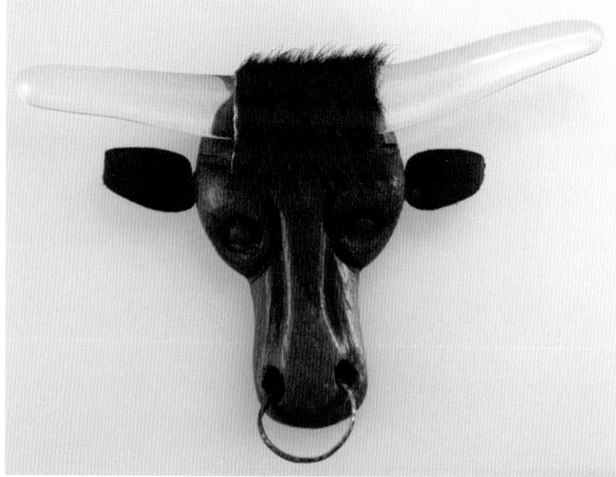

Wooden longhorn brooch, c. 1940s, carved wood with acrylic resin horns, leather ears and cowhide embellishment on the forehead, purchased in New England and now residing in Texas as it should be, unmarked, horns 4 3/4" wide. **$95-$125**

Author's Collection

McClelland Barclay necklace, c. late 1930s-early 1940s, Art Deco with Art Modern influences in a typical McClelland Barclay design with sapphire blue and clear rhinestones, 15" long. **$250-$350**

Jewelry courtesy ChicAntiques.com

Wooden basket brooch, c. 1940s, cellulose acetate flowers in white, reddish pink, and yellow mounted in carved wooden basket with green painted accents on the leaves, "C" closure with no safety catch, 2 3/4" x 2 3/4". **$65-$95**

Jewelry courtesy ChicAntiques.com

Lightning bolt brooch, c. 1940s, unfoiled stones in blue, green, and red with clear accents, marked Sterling. **$125-$150**

Jewelry courtesy ChicAntiques.com

Jelly belly deer brooch, c. 1940s, sterling silver with gold wash, Lucite belly with rhinestone eye accents, marked Sterling. **$125-$150**

Jewelry courtesy ChicAntiques.com

Forbidden Fruits lemon set, c. late 1940s, Lucite with yellow rhinestones and metal leaves lightly washed with green, brooch just under 2" including the stem; earrings 1 1/8" long; Forbidden Fruits were originally sold on paper cards bearing this name. **$75-$95**

Jewelry courtesy ChicAntiques.com

Korda fortuneteller brooch, c. 1940, made in conjunction with the movie "Thief of Bagdad" by Alexander Korda; marked Thief of Bagdad Korda (although the piece was made by Rice-Weiner), 2 1/2" long. **$150-$200**

Jewelry courtesy ChicAntiques.com

Infantry sweetheart pin, c. mid-1940s, sterling silver crossed rifles with mother of pearl heart dangling below. **$50-$75**

Jewelry courtesy ChicAntiques.com

"Old Glory" brooch, c. early 1940s, red and blue enameling with clear rhinestones. **$125-$150**

Jewelry courtesy ChicAntiques.com

LEFT Sultan brooch, c. 1940s, sterling silver set with large teal rhinestone in turban and turquoise bead accents like those used in Eisenberg jewelry, although this piece is not a Ruth Kamke design, marked Sterling; earrings missing. **$225-$325**

Jewelry courtesy ChicAntiques.com

ABOVE Boucher sterling brooch set, c. 1948, patented design with red rhinestones and clear accents, sterling silver with gold wash, marked MB (old mark with Phrygian cap), brooch 2 1/8" wide. **$300-$400**

Jewelry courtesy LinsyJsJewels.com

1950s

COSTUME JEWELRY THROUGH THE DECADES

A phrase that comes up often to describe 1950s costume jewelry is "fabulously fake" and with good reason. The pent-up demand for post-World War II consumer goods spilling over after 1940s rationing was avidly reflected in adornment, and bold statements were made in rhinestones and metalwork alike. Once the decade got into full swing, realistic-looking costume jewelry of the 1930s and 1940s was largely a thing of the past with only a few exceptions.

For evening wear, bold rhinestone necklace, bracelet, and earring designs, often sold in sets or *parures* (pronounced pah-rurs) of three or more matched pieces, dominated. Even the less sparkling jewelry for daywear, such as copper art jewelry, varied plastics, and colorful multi-strands of beads, could turn a plain frock into a polished outfit. Yes, there were more sedate pieces made and advertised by Trifari, Coro, Kramer and others, especially in the early 1950s, but what avid collectors seek today are often the bold creations that were frankly fake.

Jewelry colors in this decade ran the gamut, with clear rhinestones leading the way, but there are some other prevailing influences. For instance, baby blue rhinestones, marketed by Weiss as "ice blue" in 1953 and used in a wide range of designs, are indicative of the early 1950s in everything from simple chokers to elaborate collars and wide bracelets. In 1955, Swarovski introduced the iridescent aurora borealis stone in varying colors and literally changed jewelry history as manufacturers embraced the exciting burst of sparkle newly available to them.

Opaque white jewelry was extremely popular in the 1950s as well. Many brands marketed white pieces at varying price points, with Trifari and Kramer allotting advertising dollars to promote them in full-page magazine campaigns. For many years, collectors shunned vintage pieces in this snowy hue. Dealers avoided stocking them in their inventories despite their wardrobe versatility – they looked as beautiful in winter when worn with black as they did with summer fashions. This is still true to some extent regarding chalk white pieces, especially with lower-end jewelry. However, there is an ongoing demand for certain pieces by Schreiner and other high-end manufacturers.

The aforementioned copper jewelry also saw a surge in popularity in the 1950s. This movement was started by Frank Rebajes, who began expressing his artistic skill in copper in the 1930s before Renoir of California was founded in 1946. As a reflection of the demand for mid-century modern design, the futuristic wearable art made by these companies fed the demand for top-notch jewelry of this sort. From 1948 to 1951, Renoir jewelry was marked "Hand Made, Renoir of California" and then after simply "Renoir." Matisse, the brand stamped on Renoir of California's enameled lines, was introduced in 1952. Rebajes also made jewelry in white metal, as did Renoir for its Sauteur line, but in very limited quantities

Regency art glass brooch, c. 1950s, blue art glass stones with light and medium blue rhinestones in gold-tone setting, marked Regency, 2 3/4" long. **$85-$110**

Jewelry courtesy ChicAntiques.com

compared to its copper wares. Other companies such as Kim Craftsmen made similar copper jewelry during the 1950s as well.

As for earring styles, clips were all the rage during this decade. Clustered bead earrings to match multi-strand necklaces were prolific. These range from lightweight "made in Japan" versions wired to inexpensive filigree backings to Schiaparelli's more substantially crafted earrings with molded backings. From chandeliers to daring styles that covered the entire ear, nearly all costume jewelry earrings manufactured during this decade were clips.

Miriam Haskell's bead and pearl cluster jewelry became extremely popular during this decade, and other companies made similar designs. Jonné, Original by Robért, DeMario, and Eugene are all brands that made similar looks to Haskell's hand-manipulated designs incorporating rose montee rhinestones. All of these are quite beautiful, but Haskell's workmanship usually trumps that of similar brands when compared side by side.

Christian Dior and Hollycraft were among the brands that dated jewelry as part of their marking process during this decade. Dior's dated pieces actually span the late 1950s through the 1970s. Hollycraft began as Hollywood Jewelry Co. in the 1940s, but the pieces marked Hollycraft with 1950s dates are among the most popular with collectors.

Other friendly competitors with Hollycraft were Florenza and ModeArt, the latter of which produced most of its jewelry under the brand ART. Florenza and ART pieces have a similar look, often with modernized Victorian revival elements, and most of the jewelry made by these two firms was marked.

And in spite of reports to the contrary circulating on the Internet, no verifiable evidence has been produced thus far connecting pieces of the same period marked HAR, the mark of Hargo Creations, with those marked ART.

Also, Sphinx was not associated with Boucher or Schreiner. Sphinx, which was established in the United Kingdom in 1950, has been confirmed as making jewelry for Kenneth Jay Lane, Butler & Wilson, and department stores such as Neiman Marcus and Bloomingdale's, however. Some of this British company's pieces are only marked with design numbers.

Jewelry imported from Austria was also extremely popular during this era. These pieces employ Austrian crystal rhinestones, naturally, so their sparkle is unsurpassed. Some pieces are marked with only a crown symbol or with a crown in addition to "Austria" or "Made in Austria." These are attributed to the firm Schoffel. Even when not marked, the construction is often intricate and distinctive (see Section Three for examples). And while there has been no definite connection confirmed, some Schreiner of New York pieces from this decade bear many similar design characteristics and components to those made in Austria.

Home jewelry parties became popular during the 1950s and continued into the 1960s, with the direct selling concepts of Judy Lee and Sarah Coventry leading the way. Emmons jewelry, a sister company of Sarah Coventry, was also sold at home parties during this era. Many collectors seek these brands, and because this jewelry was so widely distributed across the United States in large quantities it is still plentiful on the secondary market. This makes the price point affordable for budget-conscious collectors in most instances, especially with Sarah Coventry.

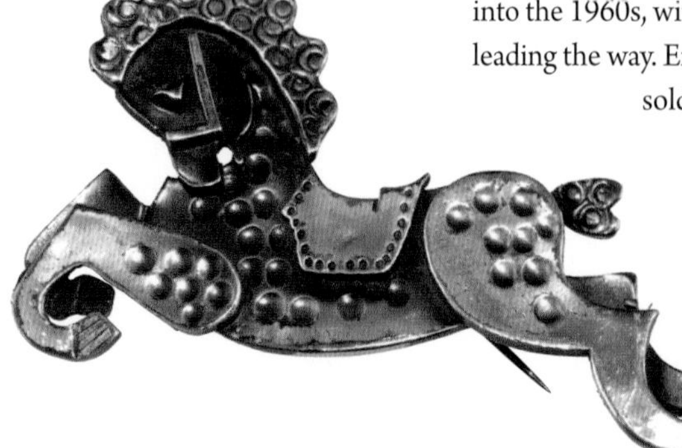

Rebajes hobby horse brooch, c. early 1950s, shown in silver-tone metal, also produced more commonly in copper, marked Rebajes, 2 7/8" long.
$125-$175 as shown

Courtesy of ChicAntiques.com

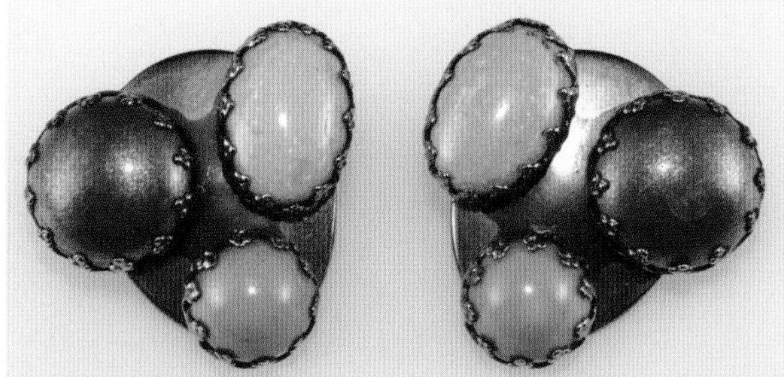

ABOVE Original by Robért Red brooch, c. late 1950s, red and pink rhinestones with gold-tone findings on a filigree backing, marked Original by Robért, 2 1/4" wide. **$225-$275**

Jewelry courtesy ChicAntiques.com

Matisse "Scarab" cuff bracelet and earrings, c. late 1950s, inspired by Egyptian scarabs, the "stones" in these pieces are actually enamel over copper, all pieces marked "Matisse," cuff 1 1/2" wide, earrings 1 1/4". **$75-$125**

Courtesy of ChicAntiques.com

Renoir "Flame" cuff bracelet and earrings, c. 1950s, marked Renoir, bracelet 1" wide, earrings 1 5/8" long. **$75-$125**

Author's Collection

And, of course, we couldn't leave the 1950s without mentioning the ubiquitous "June Cleaver" pearls that every female, from adolescent to adult, owned during this decade. Many of these faux pearl strands were high quality, and some even had elaborately rhinestoned clasps. While these hold very little value to collectors unless they are attributed to a couture house or identified as another high-end brand, they make wonderful, wearable heirlooms when passed from generation to generation.

ABOVE Alice Caviness brooch, c. 1950s, brown brilliantly faceted rhinestones surrounded by darker brown and brown/blue bicolor rhinestones, marked Alice Caviness, 2 3/8" wide. **$125-$175**

Author's Collection

Original by Robért pearl brooch, c. 1950s, simulated pearls and rhinestones clustered on gold-tone filigree backing with original foil hangtag, marked Original by Robért, 2" wide. **$125-$150**

Jewelry courtesy ChicAntiques.com

RIGHT Hinged cuff bracelet, c. 1950s, double hinge cuff with large rock-shaped pink stones surrounded by pale purple and ice blue rhinestones set in silver-tone metal, unmarked, 2" wide. **$525-$625**

Author's Collection

Schauer Fifth Avenue bracelet, c. late 1950s, opalescent glass surrounded by lavender, pale yellow, and aurora borealis rhinestones in gunmetal setting, marked Schauer Fifth Avenue, just under 7" long. **$225-$275**

Author's Collection

Austrian necklace, c. 1950s, green and peacock blue navettes with round medium blue rhinestone accents set in japanned metal, marked Austria, adjusts to 16" long, centerpiece 3" wide. **$475-$575**

Author's Collection

Florenza starfish set, c. 1950s, brown, olive green, pale blue, and clear rhinestones in antiqued gold-tone settings, marked Florenza, brooch 3" wide, earrings 1 1/2" wide. **$95-$125**

Jewelry courtesy ChicAntiques.com

Hollycraft bracelet, c. 1955, aurora borealis rhinestones set in antique gold-tone hinged clamper bracelet, marked Hollycraft Copr. 1955, 1" wide. **$135-$165**

Jewelry courtesy ChicAntiques.com

Hollycraft pink bow brooch, c. 1951, pink baguette and navette rhinestones in gold-tone setting, marked Hollycraft Copr. 1951, 2 1/2" wide. **$65-$95**

Jewelry courtesy ChicAntiques.com

Regency brooch set, c. 1950s, art glass teardrop dangles with brilliant teal green and peacock blue rhinestones in japanned setting, marked Regency Jewels on brooch, Regency on earrings, brooch 2 1/2" long, earrings 1 1/8" wide. **$125-$150**

Author's Collection

Regency bracelet, c. 1950s, green oval foiled cabochons with pastel yellow and green rhinestones in brass-tone metal, marked Regency, 7" long. **$125-$150**

Author's Collection

Original by Robért necklace, c. 1950s, simulated pearls with pink and purple rhinestones clustered on gold-tone filigree backing with clear rose montee and gold vine accents, marked Original by Robért, 16" long, centerpiece 2 1/2" wide. **$200-$250**

Jewelry courtesy ChicAntiques.com

Hollycraft foiled cabochon set, c. 1958, "cat's eye" foiled cabochons with green aurora borealis rhinestones set in antiqued gold-tone metal, marked Hollycraft Copr. 1958.
$155-$185

Jewelry courtesy ChicAntiques.com

Florenza Maltese cross set, c. 1950s, purple, blue, and aurora borealis rhinestones set in antiqued silver-tone metal, marked Florenza, pendant 2 1/2" wide, bracelet 7 1/4" long, earrings 1 1/8". **$175-$225**

Jewelry courtesy ChicAntiques.com

Alice Caviness brooch set, c. late 1950s, gray, clear, and aurora borealis rhinestones set in gold-tone metal, marked Alice Caviness, brooch 2 1/2" wide, earrings 1 1/2" long. **$175-$225**

Author's Collection

1960s

COSTUME JEWELRY THROUGH THE DECADES

When looking at jewelry from decade to decade, the early and late periods of the 1960s offer two distinct perspectives on fashion and adornment. The beginning of the decade was most certainly a carryover of the 1950s. Fashions were similar in many instances with bubble dresses and sleek sheath styles modeled by many American women. In terms of jewelry, numerous rhinestone pieces were still being made by companies such as DeLizza & Elster along with many others, and we saw Kenneth Jay Lane introduce his magnificent earring designs during this decade. Jewelry study of this period reflects a continuation of fab and fake, but there are decidedly more sedate looks that were made at this time as well.

Tailored pieces featuring simple pearl styles with gold-tone metal – especially brushed finishes – became very popular along with the ubiquitous "circle" pin worn on Jackie Kennedy-style suits early in the decade. Some were decorated with a smattering of faux pearls or clear rhinestones, but in collecting terms these are not highly desirable.

What collectors deem as "granny" beads today were also a stylish carryover from the 1950s in updated colors made by Coro, Laguna, Marvella, and others. They were so popular, in fact, that women owned them in a rainbow of colors, and many grandmothers continued to wear them well past their prime. They've had a revival in recent years with more of them

Mimi Di N geometric brooch, c. 1960s, matte gold-tone metal with four large pear-shaped clear rhinestones, designed by Mimi di Nascemi, marked Mimi Di N, 3 1/4" wide. **$200-$250**

Jewelry courtesy LinsyJsJewels.com

Cellulose acetate flower brooch, c. 1960s, pink cellulose acetate with flat-back rhinestones in center, unmarked, 3" wide. **$65-$95**

Jewelry courtesy ChicAntiques.com

Knight in Shining Armor brooch, c. 1960s, enameled brooch with embossed metal shield, unmarked, 3" wide.
$65-$95

Jewelry courtesy ChicAntiques.com

selling on the secondary market than in past decades. Crystal beads in single and multi-strands were this decade's answer to simple strands of pearls, and many of these vintage necklaces are available today at reasonable prices.

A number of companies embraced a fascination with jewels of the Far East and India. Weiss widely advertised its "India Inspired" collections that featured molded rock-shaped stones in jewel colors of green, blue, and red. Trifari and K.J.L. also marketed designs influenced by the styles of India and in themes reflecting the Orient, and these are very desirable now.

Italian designers Coppola e Toppo made some of the most fabulous beaded jewelry produced during the 1960s, using both glass and plastic components within the same over-the-top necklaces, bracelets, and earring designs. These pieces were sometimes souvenirs from European vacations, especially the more sedate cluster-style earrings. The larger, more expressive pieces are highly valued by collectors today.

Lea Stein began making jewelry reminiscent of Art Deco styles in Paris during the 1960s, using sheets of cellulose acetate, a form of plastic first used in jewelry manufacture during the 1930s. She continued working in this medium through the early 1980s before closing her business. She later reopened and is still producing imaginative and colorful figural jewelry in limited quantities using the same techniques and materials. It is difficult to tell the old jewelry from the newer, since many of the same styles were made for many years. All the older designs were animals, so designs depicting people fall into the newer category.

Celebrities starring in early 1960s movies were still costumed in memorable jewelry. Roles like Audrey Hepburn's portrayal of the bejeweled Holly Golightly in "Breakfast at Tiffany's" continued to glamorize rhinestones. A few years later Hepburn teamed up with Rex Harrison in "My Fair Lady," prompting Napier to produce both an Eliza Doolittle pin and rhinestone umbrella pins and earrings inspired by the movie. BSK made an entire collection of jewelry commemorating this film, including pins and cufflinks, prompting collectors to gather entire sets.

Colors changed in this decade, following trends in home furnishings and fashion. More olive greens, oranges, and varied earthy shades of brown were used in rhinestone and beaded jewelry, especially as the decade wore on. Twiggy's pouty May 1967 cover of French *Vogue* saw her sporting orange-red enameled butterfly pins, most likely of the fine jewelry variety, but certainly indicative of what the stylish woman would be wearing that year in costume versions. Then came the mod looks later in the 1960s with swirling enamels and beaded jewelry with hot pink, green, bright yellow, and other psychedelically vivid "tie-dyed" hues.

Rebellious youth began to revert to pierced earrings that had been unfashionable since the 1890s when they were deemed "barbaric." In the mid-1960s, young women rejected the clips of their mother's generation and shunned the ear screws of their grandmother's. Companies like Kim Craftsmen sold pierced earrings like wildfire in department store kiosks across the nation. There were even clip earrings made to simulate pierced earrings for the girl who wanted to be bad, but only on occasion. She could enjoy the pierced look without actually defacing her ears by donning those modified clips.

For the most part, the use of rhinestones waned late in the decade, and matched sets of jewelry, or parures, fell out of fashion as mixing and matching became more popular. More metalwork was seen, as was thicker gold-tone plating like that found in many Christmas jewelry items dating to the 1960s. Natural elements such as leather, fabric, wood, and feathers were also widely incorporated in jewelry as part of the hippie movement later in the decade.

Body jewelry, also innovatively introduced by Kim Craftsmen, offered unique forms of adornment, including metal bras referenced as "bumper guards." DeLizza & Elster and Napier, among others, also marketed elaborate belts incorporating rhinestones with metalwork. Napier called its draping styles "bikini belts."

Bib necklace set, c. 1960s, green, orange, and yellow rhinestones with dangling beads in complementary colors, necklace 15 1/2" long with front drop of about 3", earrings 2".
$125-$150

Jewelry courtesy ChicAntiques.com

Green rock bracelet set, c. 1960s, emerald green glass rock stones with brilliant spring green rhinestones in gold-tone setting with toggle clasp, bracelet 7 1/2" long x 1" wide, earrings 1" long. **$125-$150**

Author's Collection

Santa pins, c. 1960s, thick enameling on heavily gold-plated metal with rhinestone accents, Santa with pack of toys marked Hollycraft, others unmarked, range in height from 1 1/2" to 2 1/4" long. **$35-$65 each**

Author's Collection

De Lillo earrings, c. 1960s, large spring green teardrop rhinestones surrounded by clear accents, marked Wm. de Lillo, 1 1/2" long. **$100-$125**

Jewelry courtesy ChicAntiques.com

Boucher convertible flower brooch, c. early 1960s, flower head opens and closes to reveal simulated pearl inside, accented with clear rhinestones, marked ©Boucher, 4 1/4" long. **$200-$275**

Jewelry courtesy LinsyJsJewels.com

Original by Robért candle Christmas tree pin, c. 1960s, decorated with red and green baguette rhinestones along with clear accents, marked Original by Robért, 2 1/2" long. **$125-$175**

Jewelry courtesy ChicAntiques.com

Monet bib necklace, c. 1960s, lacy gold-plated metal pieces linked together in a bib style, adjusts to 17" long, bib 4" long in front. **$125-$150**

Jewelry courtesy ChicAntiques.com

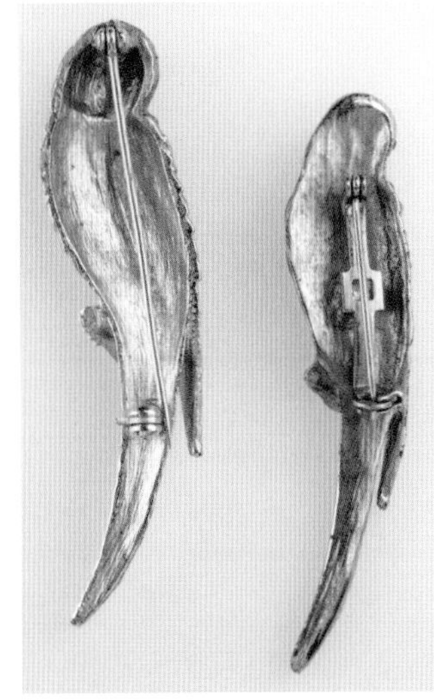

Enameled bird pins, c. 1960s, colorful enameling and rhinestone accents, 1930s look from the front, but the back view shows brushed metalwork indicative of the 1960s (see pot metal parrot pin in 1930s section for comparison), green/blue pin just over 2 3/4" long, yellow/coral pin 2 3/4" long. **$35-$45 each**

Author's Collection

Mimi Di N brooch, c. 1960s, matte gold-tone embossed metal with baroque pearl center and emerald green, fuchsia, and clear rhinestones, designed by Mimi di Nascemi, marked Mimi Di N, 3 1/4" wide. **$150-$200**

Jewelry courtesy ChicAntiques.com

Alice Caviness necklace set, c. 1960s, molded glass frosted amber stones with brown and purple aurora borealis rhinestone accents, all pieces marked Alice Caviness. **$175-$250**

Jewelry courtesy ChicAntiques.com

Rhinestone necklace set, c. 1960s, orange, olive green, and pale yellow oval rhinestones with emerald green accent stones, likely of European origin, necklace adjusts to 16 1/2", earrings 1 1/8" long. **$170-$225**

Jewelry courtesy ChicAntiques.com

Flower brooch, c. 1960s, enameled metal in black and gold, unmarked, 2 3/4" diameter. **$45-$65**

Jewelry courtesy ChicAntiques.com

Alice Caviness brooch, c. 1960s, large black glass center stone surrounded by gold-tone metalwork with orange rhinestones and clear accents, marked Alice Caviness, measurements unavailable. **$100-$125**

Jewelry courtesy ChicAntiques.com

1970s

COSTUME JEWELRY THROUGH THE DECADES

More gold-tone jewelry with few stones or other embellishments was designed in the early 1970s, but these were still large and with mod influences carried over from the 1960s. Collar-style metal chokers, with or without pendants and embellishments, were wardrobe staples.

Other carryovers from the prior decade included a continued interest in astrology, prompting many to ask the clichéd question, "What's your sign?" Jewelry worn to freely display zodiac signs served as conversation starters in many settings early in the decade.

Some of the most successful styles during this period were large pendants on chains of varied lengths in a multitude of designs at varying price points. Chain jewelry, in fact, was prolific in the 1970s in both fine and costume jewelry varieties.

The first José Barrera jewelry to get widespread attention appeared on the cover of *Vogue* in 1970. He and Maria moved to New York in 1973 and began working together under the José and Maria Barrera brand. Their lines were featured in other prominent fashion publications, and their jewelry became even more prolific in the 1980s. They are still creating high quality contemporary jewelry sold via Neiman Marcus.

Women's Wear Daily featured the designs of Willie Woo, Diane Love, and Alexis Kirk in 1971. Many of Woo's designs were nearly exact copies of 1930s pot metal pieces but were marked Willie Woo, molded into the metal, and the back construction was a bit different in comparison.

Among collectors, Love is best known for her designs for Trifari, inspired by ancient artifacts. She toured the country introducing the collection in major department stores. The jewelry itself was marked Trifari, but a paper hangtag attached to each piece identified it as a Love design. Research using jewelry advertising shared online can help collectors identify these bold pieces.

Alexis Kirk also designed some remarkably bold jewelry early in the decade, and his first commercial collection won him the Coty American Fashion Critics' Award in 1971. He was well known for including ethnic symbols, such as hamsa and Italian good luck charms along with East Indian and Asian motifs, in elaborate necklaces and brooches. His early work was owned by many celebrities including Peter Max, Jacqueline Kennedy Onassis, and the Duchess of Windsor.

The mid-'70s also saw another Egyptian revival movement in jewelry production when the treasures of King Tut toured the United States. A number of companies made jewelry to coincide with this event, including Miriam Haskell's acclaimed collection designed by Lawrence Vrba. The United States' bicentennial also inspired jewelry with historical themes, reflecting the founding fathers and other symbols of the American Revolution, along with red, white, and blue components.

Perhaps the most familiar jewelry of the disco era was spawned by the 1977 film "Saturday Night Fever" – the scarf necklace made in abundance by

Schreiner flower brooch, c. early 1970s, white art glass flower petals with purple glass bead center and purple rhinestone accents in silver-tone setting, marked Schreiner New York, 2 1/4" wide. **$125-$150**

Author's Collection

Whiting & Davis. These necklaces were made of fabulous silver- and gold-tone metal mesh. Matching earrings and halter-tops fashioned completely of mesh were also popular during this period. Whiting & Davis marketed other jewelry, regarded as well made with quality components, although it has a limited following among collectors.

Another trend from this decade was the cuff bracelet – often very wide and crafted of hammered or textured metalwork. Cuffs in silver-, gold-, or bi-tone metal mixed and matched with a variety of necklace and earring styles throughout the decade.

Later in the 1970s, when adornment was worn at all – other than select pieces of runway jewelry shown with couture collections – it was usually tailored for professional daywear and rather nondescript. These pieces are largely overlooked by today's collector as uninteresting. Many Rhode Island jewelry factories and New York jewelry companies closed or were on the verge of closing at this time.

ABOVE Miriam Haskell necklace, c. 1970s, ceramic beads and pendant with teal and dark blue glaze suspended on brass-tone chain, marked Miriam Haskell, 16" long, pendant 2 1/2" long.
$125-$150

Jewelry courtesy ChicAntiques.com

RIGHT Miriam Haskell suite, c. 1970s, cobalt blue glass elements and gold-plated ring findings, necklace 18" long, earrings 1 1/4" and 2", brooch 2 1/4".
$1,300-$1,500

Jewelry courtesy LinsyJsJewels.com

Schreiner necklace set, c. early 1970s, amber art glass beads and cabochons with amber inverted rhinestones linked with gold-tone chain and filigree balls, marked Schreiner, necklace 25" long with 3 1/2" dangle, earrings 2" long. **$225-$275**

Author's Collection

Givenchy earrings, c. 1977, gold-plated metal with faux pearl center and clear rhinestone accents, marked Givenchy Paris New York 1977, 1" wide. **$50-$75**

Jewelry courtesy ChicAntiques.com

Monet "Princesa" necklace, c. early 1970s, lacy gold-plated pierced metalwork with East Indian influence, marked Monet, adjusts to 17 1/2" long, centerpiece 4 1/4" long.
$150-$175

Author's Collection

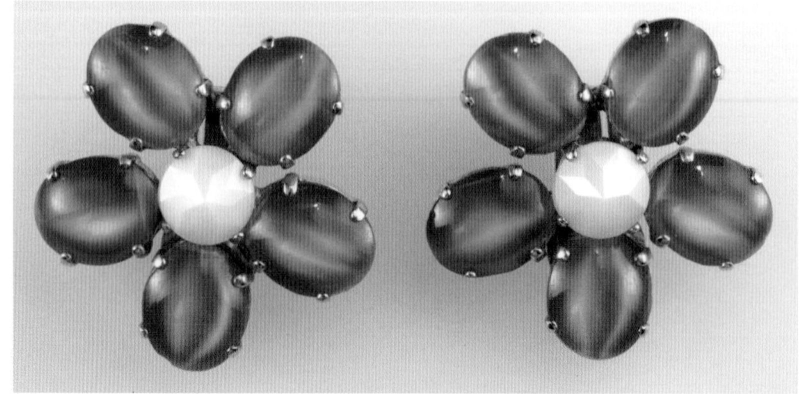

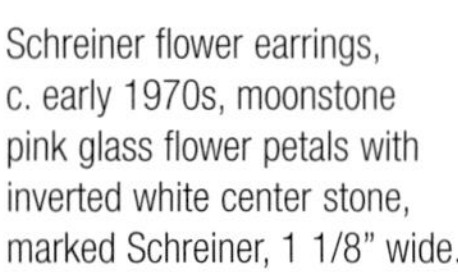

Schreiner flower earrings, c. early 1970s, moonstone pink glass flower petals with inverted white center stone, marked Schreiner, 1 1/8" wide.
$75-$100

Author's Collection

Napier dangle earrings, c. early 1970s, metal filigree hoops with heavy gold plating embellished with dangling crystal beads and metal filigree "leaf" shapes, marked Napier, over 3 1/2" long x 1 7/8" wide. **$125-$150**

Jewelry courtesy ChicAntiques.com

Chanel earrings, c. late 1970s, domed style in matte gold-tone metal, marked Chanel CC Made in France, 1" diameter. **$285-$335**

Jewelry courtesy ChicAntiques.com

Chanel CC earrings, c. late 1970s, CC logo in clear rhinestones, just over 1" diameter. **$275-$325**

Jewelry courtesy ChicAntiques.com

Napier swirl pendant, c. 1972, from the advertisement "Napier is Curlier"; silver-tone chain with large swirling pendant, marked Napier, 16 1/2" long, pendant 5 1/2" long. **$100-$150**

Author's Collection

Willie Woo palm tree pin, c. early 1970s, green enamel and clear rhinestones on pot metal setting, remake of 1930s pin, marked Willie Woo, 2" long. **$50-$65**

Author's Collection

Schreiner brooch/pendant, c. early 1970s, red and gray swirled art glass with mirror gray and black square stones in silver-tone two-piece articulated setting, pendant can be removed from chain to be worn as a brooch, marked Schreiner New York, chain 18" long, pendant 3" long. **$150-$200**

Author's Collection

Schreiner flower brooch, c. early 1970s, art glass flower petals with purple glass bead center and unfoiled inverted rhinestone accents, marked Schreiner New York, 2 3/8" wide. **$125-$150**

Author's Collection

Whiting & Davis bracelet, c. mid-1970s, hinged cuff bracelet intricately crafted of silver-tone metal with a large oval hematite-look dark gray cabochon, marked Whiting & Davis, 2 3/8" wide across the top. **$135-$165**

Jewelry courtesy ChicAntiques.com

Miriam Haskell Egyptian Revival necklace, c. 1970s, glass and ceramic scarabs and King Tut masks suspended from a metal mesh necklace with antiqued gold-tone filigree findings, marked Miriam Haskell, adjusts to 17 1/2". **$600-$750**

Jewelry courtesy ChicAntiques.com

1980s

COSTUME JEWELRY THROUGH THE DECADES

In the era of big hair and wretched excess, designer labels and logos were king. It's hard to think of the 1980s without remembering the Izod alligator and Ralph Lauren's polo pony gaining wild popularity as more fashion designers were recognized as celebrities than ever before. The emphasis was indeed on being chic and stylish as "fashion jewelry" trumped "costume jewelry" as the catch phrase denoting high-end designer wares.

Madonna's "boy toy" and "material girl" imagery emphasized adornment as a tool for self-expression. Oversized rhinestone-bedecked crosses were worn with abandon, much to the dismay of the highly religious side of the Christian community. The burgeoning music video medium allowed more young women than ever to be influenced by fashionable expression and the "punk" movement, which also embraced the wearing of rhinestone jewelry.

More than movies of the day, television dramas influenced fashion and adornment. In fact, Judith Hendler's Acri-gems, finely crafted and polished using acrylic rejects from her husband's furniture business, were discovered by Nolan Miller, costume designer for "Dynasty," when he ran into her in a Los Angeles fabric store. Joan Collins praised Hendler's work featuring signature neck rings with dangling elements, and they became staples in many 1980s wardrobes as a result of Collins wearing them on the show. Other luxury plastics were also shown in boutiques and high-end department stores in over-the-top styles. Anne and Frank Vigneri made a name for themselves by twisting and painting plastics. Their lines included many bold bracelet styles collectors still pay good sums to own today.

Chanel pearl bracelet, c. 1980s, two strands of large simulated pearls with gold-tone clasp engraved with the CC logo, crown and stylized fleur de lis, marked Chanel 2 CC 6 Made in France, just over 8 1/2" long with 1 1/4" clasp. **$575-$650**

Jewelry courtesy ChicAntiques.com

Companies like FormArt of New York introduced lavish earrings and other jewelry encrusted with Swarovski flat-backed rhinestones, which were branded as Bellini by FormArt. Richard Kerr and Barbara Groeger designed the same type of jewelry during this period. Most of these pieces have the mark encased under a resin-like material. Some Barbara Groeger earrings have metal backs, however, and were sold with stick-on labels that have worn away, leaving them unmarked today. Earrings made by these designers were most often monotone in color and are more common than bracelets and necklaces or multicolor pieces. These styles were typically bold and/or flashy, and sold in upscale boutiques and department stores. They went perfectly with Judith Leiber's whimsical jewel-covered *minaudière* evening bags that were so popular during this decade.

Fun and fanciful eyewear was introduced by Lunch at the Ritz in 1982, leading the company to develop dangling charm earrings in outlandish designs with self-explanatory names like "Chinese Takeout" and "Seafood." "Glamour, luxury and morsels of fantasy" were the goal of these kitschy designs. Many of Lunch at the Ritz's retired lines are now highly collectible, including those with holiday themes.

Wendy Gell became the queen of repurposing before repurposing was cool. She used broken bits of old jewelry combined with Swarovski crystals to create many collage masterpieces, including her highly collectible "Wristies" cuff bracelets. Her work was recognized by Oprah Winfrey and got quite a boost when featured on her television show. Gell also worked with Napier to create a line of Disney jewelry, incorporating the studio's characters into a number of varied designs.

Many American women began following the lead of the First Lady by wearing multi-strand "Barbara Bush" pearls at the end of this decade. Mrs. Bush's pearls were made by Kenneth Jay Lane, in fact. These were chunkier and bolder than Jackie Kennedy's style in the 1960s, but basically plain pearls nonetheless.

Overall, jewelry in boutiques and department stores was bold, flashy and colorful for daywear, while evening styles returned to rhinestone glitz. Jewel tones were popular as well as matte gold finishes on metalwork. Nearly every designer took a turn at producing coin jewelry, and plenty of coin was spent on adornment in turn. It was a great decade for those who loved to accessorize and the companies keeping them outfitted, but changes were most definitely on the horizon.

Wendy Gell crown brooch, c. late 1980s-early 1990s, hand-crafted collage style using rhinestones of varying shapes, sizes and colors with seed pearls and broken vintage jewelry parts, marked Wendy Gell, 15" long, front embellished plate 2 1/2" wide. **$525-$600**

Jewelry courtesy ChicAntiques.com

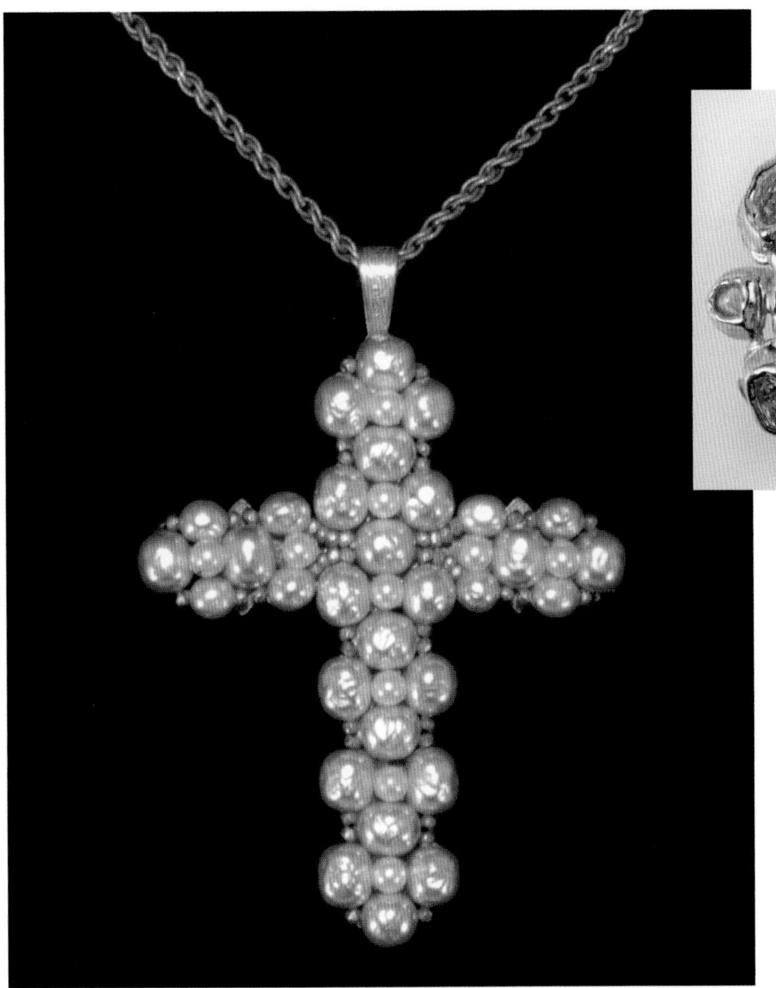

ABOVE Chanel brooch, c. 1980s, domed brooch with sparkling trapezoid clear rhinestones and Gripoix pearls in a polished gold-tone setting with European trombone clasp, marked Chanel 2 CC 9 Made in France, just over 3" wide. **$550-$625**

Jewelry courtesy ChicAntiques.com

LEFT Miriam Haskell cross necklace, c. early 1980s, simulated baroque pearls and antique gold-tone seed beads on chain, marked Miriam Haskell, cross 2 3/4" long. **$225-$275**

Jewelry courtesy ChicAntiques.com

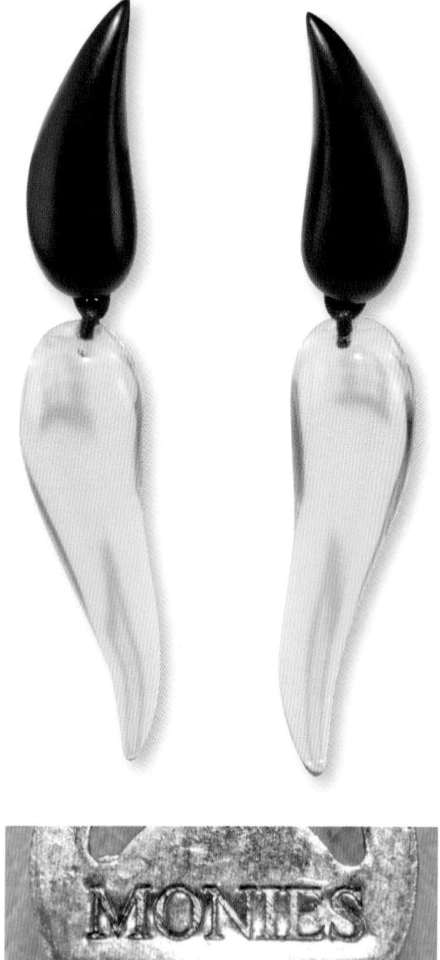

Monies earrings, c. 1980s, wood and acrylic resin joined by cord designed by Gerda Lynggaard, marked Monies. **$100-$150**

Jewelry courtesy ChicAntiques.com

Judith Hendler pink necklacc set, c. 1980s, Acri-Gems necklace made of pink acrylic, prism pendant suspended from signature neck ring with matching pierced earrings, unmarked, prism 4 3/4" long, earrings 2 1/4". **$425-$500**

Courtesy of ChicAntiques.com

Simone Edouard star earrings, c. 1980s, gold-tone backings encrusted with clear rhinestones in round elongated navette and trillion shapes, marked Simone Edouarde, 3" long. **$125-$150**

Author's Collection

Richard Kerr earrings, c. 1980s, star shapes encrusted with pink Swarovski flat-back crystals, marked Richard Kerr, 1 7/8" wide. **$75-$95**

Jewelry courtesy ChicAntiques.com

Barbara Groeger earrings, c. 1980s, red and black flat-backed rhinestones in target and dots patterns, marked Barbara Groeger, 3 1/2" long. **$125-$150**

Jewelry courtesy ChicAntiques.com

ABOVE Chanel dangle earrings, c. 1980s, simulated pearls in heavy gold-tone clip back settings, marked Chanel CC Made in France, 3 1/2" long.
$475-$550

Jewelry courtesy ChicAntiques.com

RIGHT Charm necklace, c. late 1980s, matte gold-tone chain with dangling charms, some with rhinestone embellishments, unmarked, purchased and worn by the author in the late 1980s, 17" long, longest charm 1 1/4".
$50-$75

Author's Collection

Karl Lagerfeld earrings, c. 1980s, stylized fleur de lis tops with dangling faux pearls, marked KL in script, 1 3/8" long.
$75-$100

Jewelry courtesy ChicAntiques.com

Wendy Gell necklace, c. 1985, hand-crafted collage necklace using faux pearls and rhinestones of varying shapes and sizes along with broken vintage jewelry parts, marked Wendy Gell 1985, 15" long, front embellished plate 2 1/2" wide. **$325-$400**

Jewelry courtesy ChicAntiques.com

1990s

COSTUME JEWELRY THROUGH THE DECADES

To say that jewelry design did an about-face in the 1990s is not an exaggeration. A few companies produced bold lines in the early 1990s, like Napier and Monet, but that tapered off dramatically as the decade proceeded. It was as if history was repeating the boring late-1970s as styles shrank into demure understatements or disappeared completely from red carpets and runways. The minimalist movement was back in a big way as far as the fashion jewelry industry was concerned.

About the same time, vintage costume jewelry was really heating up as a collectible genre. Yesterday's "junk jewelry" was even more desirable to collectors than it was to the women who owned it when it was new, and was certainly more in demand than it was just decades earlier when pieces were being broken apart to use for craft projects. Books were being published on the topic, organizations were forming to encourage collecting pursuits, and jewelry designers of the past were enjoying a renaissance as celebrities by those who appreciated their vintage work.

While jewelry in department stores may have been uninteresting, some of those designers and others inspired by them were creating masterpieces on a small scale that had a huge impact among collectors. One of these talented men was Lawrence Vrba, who had worked for Miriam Haskell and Castlecliff in the 1970s.

Vrba hand crafted jewelry in oversized styles featuring Haskellesque pearls along with flower vases, glass leaves, and a plethora of rhinestone shapes and sizes – basically anything that inspired him – and collectors took notice in the 1990s. His large Christmas tree pins were an instant hit along with everything else bearing his oval name plaque. His impact on costume jewelry collecting and his contributions to the community were honored in 2013 with the first-ever CJCI Achievement Award presented by Costume Jewelry Collectors International. He was also awarded the 2013 TDF/Irene Sharaff Artisan Award for his theatrical jewelry designs. He is still crafting beautiful jewelry, and more of his later designs are included in the 2000s section of this guide.

Dom DeToro began designing under the Dominique brand in the 1990s, although some of his earlier pieces were unmarked. He utilized skills honed while crafting jewelry for a company that supplied both Weiss and Eisenberg in the 1950s. His lavishly large rhinestone butterfly brooches were discovered for sale in a Rhode Island antiques store in the mid-1990s, just as collectors were beginning to notice his vintage-style work and started seeking out his pieces. He made jewelry well into his late 80s, retiring in 2010.

Dorothy Bauer's capricious jewelry, which began as "A Piece of the Rainbow" in 1982, was also very popular in the 1990s when many of

Elizabeth Taylor "Eternal Flame" earrings, c. 1993, glass ruby cabochon base with faux turquoise ovals and pavé set clear rhinestones mimicking fine jewelry from Elizabeth Taylor's legendary collection, marked Elizabeth Taylor Avon, 1 5/8" long.
$150-$200

Jewelry courtesy ChicAntiques.com

Elizabeth Taylor Egyptian earrings, c. 1993, Egyptian Revival earrings created by Avon based on fine jewelry from Elizabeth Taylor's legendary collection, turquoise blue enamel with faux lapis and turquoise cabochons on matte gold-tone metal, excellent quality, marked Elizabeth Taylor Avon, 3" long. **$150-$200**

Jewelry courtesy ChicAntiques.com

Vrba vase brooch, c. late 1990s, miniature vase with Chinese motif embellished with glass leaves, yellow glass flowers, turquoise and yellow glass beads, and faux pearls with clear rhinestone accents, marked Lawrence Vrba, 5 3/4" long. **$425-$500**

Author's Collection

Miriam Haskell dangle pearl brooch, c. late 1990s, simulated baroque pearls and rose montee rhinestones with faux pearl seed beads wired to classic Haskell filigree findings, marked Miriam Haskell, 2 1/2" long. **$250-$275**

Jewelry courtesy ChicAntiques.com

her limited edition Christmas designs were manufactured. These can be quite expensive to add to a collection now, and holiday jewelry enthusiasts relish them. Her business operated through 2007.

Bettina von Walhof also made the collectible jewelry circuit of the day selling extra large figurals completely crafted of colorful rhinestones. Earlier pieces are marked "Bettina von Walhof" on an oval cartouche. Her daughter, Michelle, continued her legacy into the 2000s, signing the later jewelry "B&M von Walhof" in a heart-shaped plaque. Various dog breeds and vintage-style brooches with holiday themes were some of their specialties.

And, of course, the couture houses including Chanel, Valentino, and others continued to make jewelry to show with their clothing collections during the 1990s. These pieces, for the most part, were not viewed as collectible until very recently. Logo enthusiasts seek jewelry from any era today as long as it is prominently branded, while avid collectors look at the components and craftsmanship that went into the making of each piece.

As for what's "vintage" and what's not, the cutoff for some online sellers is a sliding scale of 20 years and older dictated by the venues where they sell. If you go by that benchmark, jewelry from the early 1990s is now vintage. Many purists still don't see it that way, however. They're doing well to include pieces from the 1970s, and even those have to be really special pieces. Other costume jewelry worthy of note from the 1980s and 1990s is deemed "collectible."

BELOW Elizabeth Taylor "Gilded Age" earrings, c. 1993, glass ruby cabochons with faux pearls in matte gold-tone settings with cherub motif inspired by fine jewelry from Elizabeth Taylor's legendary collection, marked Elizabeth Taylor Avon, 2" long.
$175-$225

Jewelry courtesy ChicAntiques.com

LEFT Pierre Balmain heart brooch, c. early 1990s, polished gold-tone metal with black enamel and pavé set clear rhinestones, marked Pierre Balmain, 2 3/4" wide.
$100-$125

Jewelry courtesy ChicAntiques.com

ABOVE Dominique butterfly brooch, c. mid-1990s, large brooch by Dom DeToro comprised of red, clear, and opaque black rhinestones in silver-tone setting, marked Dominique, 4 5/8" wide.
$275-$375

Author's Collection

Bauer Christmas tree pin with removable base, c. late 1990s, multicolor rhinestones with display base that unscrews, marked Bauer (and numbered as a limited edition with hand engraving), 3 1/4" long. **$350-$450**

Jewelry courtesy ChicAntiques.com

BELOW Lunch at the Ritz Santa pin/pendant, c. late 1990s-early 2000s, enameled Santa with rhinestone embellishments, articulated so body, arms and legs move, star and pack of toys dangle from hands, marked Lunch at the Ritz, 3 1/4" long. **$125-$175**

Author's Collection

LEFT Vrba pearl set, c. 1995, Miriam Haskell-style brooch and earrings featuring baroque and round faux pearls with faceted and rose montee clear rhinestones, unmarked (purchased from designer – Vrba jewelry is rarely unmarked), brooch 2 1/2" wide, earrings 1 3/8" wide. **$300-$375**

Author's Collection

RIGHT Bauer limited edition Christmas tree pin, c. late 1990s, rivolis, melon molded glass, and varied rhinestones in fuchsia, teal green, and clear with frosted glass base, marked Bauer (and numbered with hand engraving), 3 1/4" long. **$250-$350**

Jewelry courtesy ChicAntiques.com

ABOVE Bettina von Walhof Santa brooch, c. late 1990s, trembler head mounted on spring, encrusted with clear, red, green, and opaque black rhinestones, marked Bettina von Walhof, 6" tall. **$550-$675**

Author's Collection

RIGHT Chanel 2.55 handbag charm brooch, c. 1994, named 2.55 for the famous Chanel flap handbag style introduced in February 1955, gold-tone polished metal with CC coin medallion at top, marked Chanel 94 CC A made in France, 3 1/8" long. **$375-$425**

Jewelry courtesy ChicAntiques.com

2000s

COSTUME JEWELRY THROUGH THE DECADES

Costume jewelry made during the 2000s is usually described as "contemporary" by collectors, and many pieces are indeed collectible even though they're newer. Many dealers and collectors don't pay much attention to this type of jewelry, but the truth is that there is a large market for it and many folks gather beautifully crafted examples to display alongside their vintage pieces. Others seek out particular brands they love regardless of the age. An entire book could be devoted to newer jewelry with a following among collectors.

In fact, television shows like "Sex and the City" and movies like "The Devil Wears Prada" introduced a host of couture brands to the average American. Jewelry and other accessories made by Chanel, Prada, Roberto Cavalli, Rodrigo Otazu, and many others were featured on screen, and demand for these lines grew as they were collected by burgeoning fashionistas worldwide.

So what makes a contemporary jewelry example "collectible" and worth buying for good sums? There are a number of factors to consider, including craftsmanship, components used in construction, the designer who envisioned the piece, the quantity in which the item was produced, and the overall quality. If that sounds a lot like what you would consider in a vintage piece of jewelry, you're on the right track.

Whether you purchase a piece of contemporary jewelry in an upscale department store, from a website, or directly from the skilled craftsperson who made it, as a collector you want to evaluate the jewelry just as you would evaluate a vintage item. That's not to say you can't purchase trendy items from bargain boutiques and enjoy wearing them, but generic mass-market jewelry made in Asia doesn't usually qualify as contemporary collectible jewelry. As a good amount of time passes, some of those inexpensive novelty pieces and fad-driven styles may gain popularity as collectibles, but you can't expect them to be valuable in the short term.

Another thing to keep in mind about contemporary jewelry is that there are many designers and companies that have produced pieces mimicking vintage jewelry during the recent past. These types of revivals, just as we've seen and discussed throughout the decades here, are often embraced by collectors when they are stylish and nicely made. There's no question that history repeats itself in the accessories marketplace.

The downside to vintage-look jewelry is that many dealers, whether knowingly or mistakenly, market these pieces as old when they aren't. Big name mass-marketed brands like R.J. Graziano, Heidi Daus, and Sweet Romance, along with a host of smaller jewelry designers like Haley

Jarin Kasi sterling brooch, c. mid-2000s, clear specialty rhinestones and round accents in a vintage-inspired design with gunmetal plating, marked Jarin Sterling, 3" long. **$325-$450**

Jewelry courtesy ChicAntiques.com

Francoise Montague brooch, c. mid-2000s, large simulated turquoise cabochon surrounded by light brown and blue opalescent rhinestones, marked FM, 2 1/4" diameter. **$175-$225**

Jewelry courtesy ChicAntiques.com

Hill, Elizabeth Cole and Jarin Kasi, are commonly described as "vintage" by sellers because they have the look, but most of the pieces aren't technically old enough to have that distinction. The general rule of thumb these days is 20-25 years old to be considered vintage, although some people only consider jewelry from the 1970s and earlier to be deserving of this description.

Some brands that seem to readily fool marketers who aren't familiar with them are Pierre Lorion Sylvia Karels, Siman Tu, Phillipe Ferandis, Franciose Montague, and Lorren Bell. These are all names to look for, and some of their pieces are beautifully well made and collection-worthy, but the jewelry being sold as vintage by these designers is new, or at least newer, in most instances.

Brands like Lorren Bell and Marie Ferrá have been around since the early 1990s. Others like Philippe Ferandis and Lunch at the Ritz began in the 1980s, so technically early pieces made by these designers and companies are moving into the vintage realm if you abide by the 20-year rule mentioned above. Franciose Montague is an old French brand that now has a new owner carrying on the name; most of the pieces offered for sale today are new and marked with an "FM" cartouche or have a plastic and paper hangtag.

Other favorites of collectors like Lawrence Vrba, Iradj Moini, Robert Sorrell, and the Dominique brand made by Dom DeToro were also produced largely during the past 20 years. All these designers began making jewelry prior to the 2000s, but the vast majority of pieces with these marks fall into the contemporary category. Other than DeToro, who is now retired, these talented men are still marketing jewelry today, so learning about current production and design styles behooves the collector wanting to add earlier pieces to her jewelry stash. It's also worth mentioning that not all pieces featured in jewelry reference guides date to the 1990s as purported, and many online sellers represent newer pieces to be "vintage" when they know they were actually recently made.

Rodrigo Otazu necklace, c. mid-2000s, asymmetrical design using dangling heart charms with mink brown rhinestones and simulated pearls in silver-tone metal, with signature pink Otazu pouch, marked Otazu, adjusts to 17". **$150-$200**

Jewelry courtesy ChicAntiques.com

Then you have the ladies. Bettina and Michelle von Walhof continued to market jewelry under the B&M von Walhof brand through the mid- to late- 2000s. BeeGee McBride began offering custom-made handcrafted collage-style Christmas tree pins to her customers in the early 2000s. Her designs were quickly copied by Asian manufacturers, so if a piece in question isn't marked B.G. or beegee, then it's a replica. These lines are no longer being produced and definitely have their fair share of fans.

The clever Sally Hoffman introduced her Painted Lady Ltd. jewelry later in the 2000s, incorporating handmade faces she commissions and then embellishes with vintage components gleaned from broken pieces. A number of contemporary female designers are also making over-the-top rhinestone jewelry styled in the tradition of vintage that will knock your socks off, including Katerina Musetti. And because they are handcrafted one piece at a time by the designer, this jewelry is produced in limited quantities, making it highly collectible. Musetti is currently branching out into couture collections that offer bold and striking designs in unique and brilliant color combinations as well.

So what it boils down to is this: If you like the jewelry being designed and made by contemporary artisans, buy those pieces for your collection. Adornment doesn't have to be vintage to be beautiful or collectible. There are also many other trendy, low-end, imported-from-Asia jewelry items that don't fall into the collectible category but are simply fun to wear.

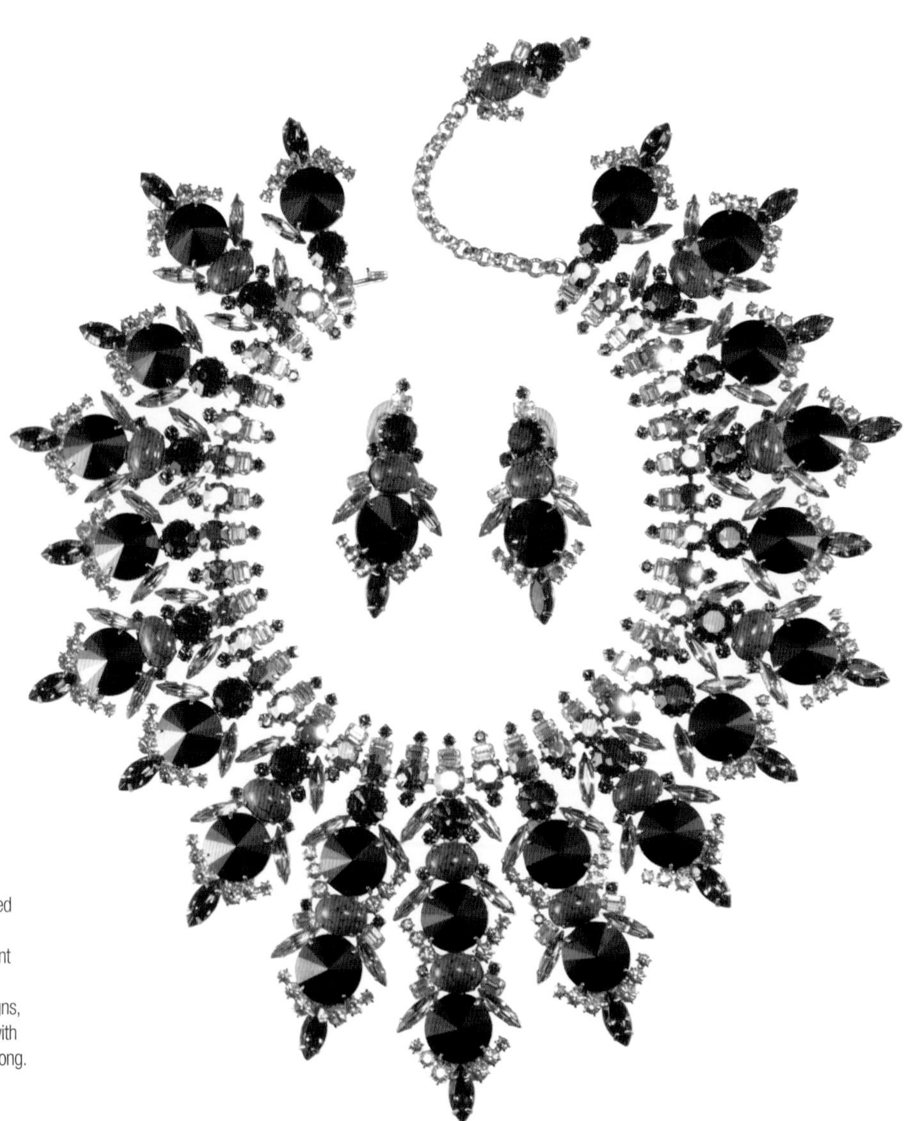

Katerina Musetti necklace set, c. 2012, collar necklace with bronze rivolis and oval simulated coral cabochons with fuchsia, lavender, and pale yellow accent rhinestones in varying shapes, marked Katerina Musetti Designs, necklace adjusts to 18" long with 4" front drop, earrings 2 1/2" long. **$850-$1,000**

Author's Collection

Dominique necklace set, c. early 2000s, collar necklace with brilliant red and clear rhinestones in silver-tone setting, marked Dominique, necklace 17 1/2" long x 1 1/2" wide, earrings 2 1/8" long. **$375-$450**

Author's Collection

Dominique butterfly brooch, c. 2000s, blue and clear rhinestones in varied shapes and sizes set in gold-tone metal, marked Dominique, 3 3/4" wide. **$245-$285**

Jewelry courtesy ChicAntiques.com

Loren Bell hinged cuff bracelet, c. mid-2000s, Art Deco-inspired design featuring clear rhinestones in gunmetal setting, 1 1/2" wide. **$150-$200**

Jewelry courtesy ChicAntiques.com

Hope Diamond replica pin/ pendant, c. 2000s, adaptation of the original Hope Diamond donated to the Smithsonian in 1958 by jeweler Harry Winston; custom-cut European glass center stone surrounded by prong-set pear-shaped and cushion-cut cubic zirconia in rhodium-plated setting, 1 5/8" wide. (Author's Note: Many variations of this pin have been made; other inferior versions have glued rather than prong-set stones.) **$75-$125**

Jewelry courtesy ChicAntiques.com

R.J. Graziano rhinestone bracelet, c. mid-2000s, round clear rhinestones in a vintage-inspired design with gunmetal plating, each rhinestone strand moves independently, marked Graziano, 7" long. **$125-$175**

Jewelry courtesy ChicAntiques.com

ABOVE Judith Hendler earrings, c. 2012, new design in black acrylic made in conjunction with the California's Designing Women exhibit at the Autry Museum in Los Angeles in 2012, marked Judith Hendler on foil sticker, 3 1/4" long. **$100-$125**

Author's Collection

LEFT Philippe Ferrandis necklace, c. late 1990s-early 2000s, Art Deco revival style with laughing Buddha made of green resin, black glass elements and beads, and rhinestone set silver-tone geometric metalwork, marked Philippe Ferrandis Paris, adjusts to 19" long with 4 3/8" front centerpiece. **$450-$525**

Author's Collection

GEMSCOPE
an in-depth look

FAR RIGHT **B&M von Walhof Valentine cat brooch, c. early 2000s, inspired by vintage Valentine cards of the 1950s; comprised of black, gray, red, and green round rhinestones, head and heart are layered, adding dimension, marked B&M von Walhof, just under 4" tall. $325-$400**

Author's Collection

RIGHT **Swarovski Rockefeller Center tree brooch, c. 2005, green navettes with multicolor rhinestones and clear accents on base and star, one of several collectible dated tree pins issued in the 2000s, marked Rockefeller Center 2005 with Swarovski swan logo. $175-$225**

Jewelry courtesy ChicAntiques.com

FAR RIGHT **Vrba skeleton brooch, c. 2006, black molded glass leaves, resin skeleton, orange rhinestones and orange cabochons in gunmetal setting, 5" long, marked Lawrence Vrba. $500-$650**

Author's Collection

RIGHT **Dominique Christmas tree brooch, c. 2000s, large red navette rhinestones with clear rhinestone garland, marked Dominique, 4" long. $175-$225**

Jewelry courtesy ChicAntiques.com

Collectible Holiday Jewelry

The wild popularity of vintage jewelry – including Christmas tree pins and other varied themes donned to show holiday spirit – has inspired many contemporary designers and manufacturers to create beautiful collectible pieces to commemorate every season.

Vrba oversized flower brooch, c. 2010, red molded glass with gray faux pearls and red and clear rhinestones in gunmetal, marked Lawrence Vrba, 5 1/4" wide. **$350-$400**

Author's Collection

Vrba Maharajah brooch, c. 2010, molded face with turquoise glass elements, faux pearls, and clear rhinestones, marked Lawrence Vrba, 5" long. **$450-$550**

Photo by Jay B. Siegel, courtesy CJCI Magazine

Vrba convertible necklace set, c. 2010, flower comprised of large pearl-finish petals, baroque pearls, and rhinestones suspended from triple strand pearl and rhinestone necklace, flower (4" wide) can be removed and worn as a brooch, marked Lawrence Vrba, necklace adjusts to 19" long. **$600-$750**

Author's Collection

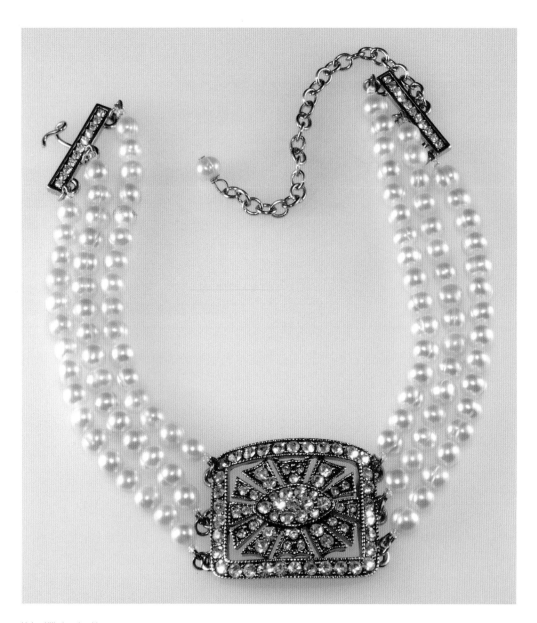

Haley Hill shoe buckle necklace, c. mid-2000s, fresh water pearls with centerpiece fashioned of gold-plated metal set with rhinestones, made with mold created from early 1900s shoe buckle, marked Haley Hill, adjusts to 16". **$150-$200**

Jewelry courtesy ChicAntiques.com

Philippe Ferrandis flower brooch, c. mid-2000s, black enameled flowers with jeweled centers, marked Philippe Ferrandis Paris. **$275-$350**

Jewelry courtesy ChicAntiques.com

ABOVE Rodrigo Otazu bracelet, c. 2000s, large glass navette moonstones surrounded with clear rhinestone overlay floret and mink brown cubic zirconia embellishments, marked Rodrigo Otazu, 1 1/2" wide. **$350-$425**

Jewelry courtesy ChicAntiques.com

Prada charm bracelet, c. mid-2000s, matte gold-tone bracelet with framed leather charms including Prada triangular logo, 7 1/4" long. **$175-$225**

Jewelry courtesy ChicAntiques.com

Section Two

DESIGNERS AND MANUFACTURERS

This section is titled "Designers *and* Manufacturers" for a reason. You've likely heard jewelry bearing some type of mark or signature referenced as "designer" jewelry. Pieces with identifying characteristics that attribute them to one company or another are also referred to in this way. But assuming that Miriam Haskell, Kenneth Jay Lane, and Albert Weiss designed every piece with their name on it is a misnomer. Some jewelry with a name attached to it was indeed designed by that individual, but that's often not the case. The jewelry may have been handcrafted, like Haskell, but not by Miriam herself. Jewelry may have been designed by an individual early on in a career, like K.J.L, but later pieces were chosen from a manufacturer's catalog and marketed bearing famous initials or a name. And then, in the case of Weiss, it's been reported that his company never manufactured jewelry, but is that true?

Jewelry manufacturers like Trifari, Coro, Napier, and many others actually employed a staff of designers who made the jewelry they sold in their own factories. Men like Trifari's Alfred Philippe and Coro's Gene Verri (shortened from Verrecchio) have been elevated to icon status among collectors. But former company executives have verified that not all Trifari designs were Philippe's during his reign, even when he signed the patent paperwork. And you'll find Adolph Katz, who was a vice president of Coro rather than a designer, with far more patents on record than Verri. That's the story that has been related from the late Mr. Verri himself.

There were also "jobbers," many of whom made jewelry for others with various nameplates attached. That's why you'll often see jewelry in the exact same styles and color combinations with the name Hattie Carnegie on one piece and Alice Caviness on another, and Hobé on yet another color combination. All these companies chose the same style produced by one jobber or another and then advertised and sold it under their names. Many of the companies using monikers related to famous designer names did business this way at some point. In fact, when examining the same jewelry found with Carnegie, Caviness, Hobé, and K.J.L. labels, among others, from the late 1960s on, this seems to be the norm rather than the exception. And to muddy the water a bit more, some unsigned pieces in the same styles were sold by jobbers to department stores so they could brand them as their house lines, using cards and boxes bearing only the retailer's name.

Truthfully, though, adding an attribution in these instances serves to identify certain styles and a level of quality as much as to pinpoint which company ordered a particular piece of jewelry from a particular jobber. The identity of most of the companies that actually made pieces for the top brands has been lost as businesses closed and records were destroyed. We're lucky to have research that shows companies like Marner and DeLizza & Elster worked for others while producing their own brands as well. Much of this unsigned jewelry is of high quality, and putting it in the designer category isn't wrong. That is, as long as you realize that purporting something as a Kenneth Jay Lane or a Hattie Carnegie design doesn't mean that these people actually designed those pieces when they were made with different brand labels attached to the same style.

And what difference does it make, really? To understand the history of collectible costume jewelry, the business end of how these items were (and still are in some cases) produced and marketed, is part of appreciating one piece over another. It's what makes an early piece actually imagined and sketched by a famous designer more rare and valuable in comparison to those later pieces simply bearing a name. Not everyone cares about collectible jewelry to this degree, but it's important to understand whether you're dating jewelry, valuing it, or garnering knowledge for your own personal satisfaction. And if you're going to market jewelry and educate others about what you're selling, knowing what you're talking about builds confidence in repeat customers.

Ciner exotic bird brooch, c. 1980s, black and coral enamel on gold-tone metal with clear and green rhinestones and simulated turquoise beads, marked Ciner, 2 3/4" long. **$175-$225**

Jewelry courtesy ChicAntiques.com

About the Designers and Manufacturers Included

Since there are far more designers and manufacturers out there than one general reference guide can include, this selection was put together to incorporate many of the most common names you're likely to run across when shopping for vintage jewelry at yard sales, flea markets, and antique malls. Including some of the Holy Grail brands that delight collectors makes a book like this one fun and entertaining, so you'll find a number of those here as well. Lastly, some designers and companies with confusing histories or misnomers associated with their jewelry are also featured in this section. You will learn more about other varied companies in Sections One and Three of the book as well.

As mentioned in the introduction to this book, costume jewelry research, like any other form of history being documented, is rather fluid. New tidbits of information gleaned from interviews with former employees, family members of company owners, news articles, advertisements, and company archives that are rediscovered, along with a host of other sources, allow jewelry historians to hone the reliable information we have available about each company, manufacturer, and jobber. We certainly don't discredit anyone hypothesizing or researching before us. Some jewelry history is based on educated guesses until those suppositions can be confirmed or discredited. Jewelry lovers realize that the advent of the Internet made more research resources available, so we can learn more about who made, sold and wore what we know now as vintage costume jewelry. That's why you may discover some new or corrected information in this book when compared to others in your reference library.

And since not every designer or manufacturer of note can be included here, a marks section at the end of this chapter serves to supplement the introductory profiles with basic information about a number of others. Many pieces from brands featured in the marks section also illustrate Section One: Jewelry Through the Decades and Section Three: Identifying and Dating in this book. It's also important to remember that quite a few "designer" pieces made by those aforementioned jobbers are not marked. You'll also learn more about distinguishing unsigned jewelry made by notable companies in recognizable styles in Section Three of this reference guide.

It's also worth noting that these brief profiles can't begin to truly encapsulate all there is to know about these designers and companies. If you find one or more that interests you, set out on a quest to learn more about that type of jewelry and enjoy the ride.

ABOVE Schiaparelli earrings, c. 1950s, textured gold-tone settings with emerald and peridot green rhinestones, marked Schiaparelli, 1 1/2" long. **$125-$150**

Jewelry courtesy ChicAntiques.com

RIGHT Eisenberg Original dress clip, c. late 1930s, jewel tone rhinestones set in pot metal with dangling glass beads in red, green, and blue below, marked Eisenberg Original, 3 1/4" long. **$550-$700**

Jewelry courtesy LinsyJsJewels.com

CARNEGIE

DESIGNERS AND MANUFACTURERS

Hattie Kanengeiser changed her name to Carnegie in the early 1900s when Andrew Carnegie was well known as the richest man alive. This was a bold move for an even bolder woman who made her mark on the fashion world with reportedly no formal training as a designer or seamstress. She died in 1956, but the fashion house bearing her name continued to do business in New York until the 1970s.

The costume jewelry portion of Carnegie's story began in 1939 when she introduced her first line. Carnegie employed Pauline Trigère, a designer with a recognizable name in the jewelry-collecting world. Prior to his own critically acclaimed success, Alexis Kirk also designed a line of jewelry reflecting his vision for artistry, which often included ethnic and supernatural symbols. This under-$5 department store line was, according to Kirk in a 1971 interview, a watered down mass-market failure. Yes, even the companies with a reputation for success had flops such as these, and some pieces bearing the Hattie Carnegie name are more beautiful than others. Although some sources indicate that the company ceased operation in 1976, others have documented jewelry designed by Yves Saint Laurent, Anne Klein, and Valentino for Carnegie in the late 1970s.

In later years, a number of different companies including DeLizza & Elster made jewelry marked with the Hattie Carnegie oval signature cartouche. You'll find many of those later designs coincide with other designer brands such as Alice Caviness, Hobé, and Kenneth Jay Lane.

Hattie Carnegie elephant necklace, c. late 1960s-early 1970s, oversized articulated pendant in gold-tone metal with green glass cabochon eye and rhinestone collar, marked Hattie Carnegie, pendant 7" long. **$225-$300**

Jewelry courtesy ChicAntiques.com

Hattie Carnegie brooch set, c. late 1950s, bicolor amber and clear glass beads dangling from a hand-manipulated brooch featuring gold-tone florets with aurora borealis rhinestones and coordinating earrings, marked Hattie Carnegie, brooch 3" wide, earrings 1 1/4". **$225-$300**

Jewelry courtesy LinsyJsJewels.com

Hattie Carnegie bracelet set, c. early 1960s, textured gold-tone chain with gold-tone bead dangles and rhinestone rondelles, matching cluster style clip earrings, marked Hattie Carnegie, bracelet 7", earrings 1 1/4". **$175-$250**

Jewelry courtesy LinsyJsJewels.com

Hattie Carnegie flower brooch set, c. 1950s, large brooch with curved petals comprised of brown, olive green, blue, and pale yellow rhinestones, matching clip earrings, marked Hattie Carnegie, brooch 3" wide, earrings 1 1/4" long.
$325-$400

Jewelry courtesy LinsyJsJewels.com

LEFT Hattie Carnegie necklace, c. 1960s, bib-style with emerald green and clear rhinestones, marked Hattie Carnegie, 16 1/2" long with a 6" drop at the front.
$375-$475

Jewelry courtesy ChicAntiques.com

ABOVE Hattie Carnegie necklace set, c. 1950s, hematite glass oval cabochons and large round givre stones in clear and white with clear, black, and aurora borealis rhinestone accents, marked Carnegie on ear clips, necklace adjusts to 16 1/2" long, earrings 1 1/2". **$225-$300**

Jewelry courtesy ChicAntiques.com

GEMSCOPE
an in-depth look

Reinad Asian Princess Brooch

One of the most famous designs marketed by Hattie Carnegie, the Asian Princess, was copied by Reinad in the early 1940s. While still a collectible period copy in its own right, the Reinad example shown here doesn't have the fine craftsmanship and quality of the Carnegie piece marked with an HC enclosed in a diamond shape designed by Ruth Kamke for Fallon & Kappel. $225-275 (See Eisenberg for more information on the design genius of Kamke and her work with Fallon & Kappel.)

There are also copies of copies in this design that were made and marketed at varied price points, the cheapest of which sold through Sears Roebuck for $1.07. Even for 1943 that's a low price and not indicative of high quality jewelry. So, in other words, if your Asian Princess isn't marked, there's no way it's the original Kamke-designed brooch produced for Hattie Carnegie. This is also a good place to note that there's no documented evidence that Reinad did work for other companies, including Carnegie, although this is purported in some reference guides. Reinad did, however, copy the designs of many others. *Jewelry courtesy ChicAntiques.com*

Hattie Carnegie brooch, c. 1950s, blue cabochons and simulated pearls with blue, lavender, and yellow rhinestones in varying shapes and sizes, marked Hattie Carnegie, 3 1/2" wide. **$175-$200**

Jewelry courtesy ChicAntiques.com

ABOVE Hattie Carnegie brooch set, c. 1950s, simulated turquoise oval cabochons, "dragon's breath" stones, red rhinestones, and aurora borealis and clear accents, marked Hattie Carnegie, brooch 2 7/8" long and 1" deep, earrings 1 1/4" wide. **$225-$300**

Jewelry courtesy ChicAntiques.com

Hattie Carnegie earrings, c. 1950s, blue cabochons and simulated pearls with blue, lavender, and yellow rhinestones, marked Carnegie, 1 3/8" wide. **$65-$85**

Jewelry courtesy ChicAntiques.com

CHANEL

DESIGNERS AND MANUFACTURERS

Vintage jewelry made by the House of Chanel never seems to lose its appeal with collectors of high-end jewelry. The earliest pieces from 1914-1939, which were unmarked, don't come on the market often today. Most of them are in museums and private collections as cherished treasures. Pieces featuring poured glass from the House of Gripoix (see Section Three for more information on Gripoix glass) to simulate gemstones are usually the most desirable and expensive, and they can also be some of the most beautiful Chanel pieces produced.

It should also be noted, in spite of many pieces appearing in well-known jewelry guides and being sold by well-known auction houses, jewelry marked with the Chanel script mark was not made by the House of Chanel. These enameled pot metal pieces were made in 1941 by Chanel Novelty Co., a division of Reinad, and they don't really measure up to Chanel standards although they are collectible in their own right. Chanel had halted production due to World War II at that point, but the fashion house sued Reinad nonetheless, and the script-marked pieces were no longer made. This information has come to light since prior references were published.

Jewelry made from 1954, when the House of Chanel reopened after World War II, through the 1960s was still largely unmarked, although there are some exceptions where a block signature or a round plaque bearing three stars were used. Famed designer Robert Goosens is credited for most of these pieces. In the 1970s a round Chanel signature plaque came about; since then, the marks and stamps used have varied through the decades.

Collectors of vintage jewelry tend to look for pieces with outstanding design, regardless of age or markings, rather than seek out the familiar CC logo. The logo encapsulating Coco Chanel's name was further popularized by Karl Lagerfeld after he began to lead this couturier's design team in 1983. The logo has increasingly become a status symbol over the past 30 years, with many celebrities spurring the trend by posing for photographs wearing Chanel jewelry. Interestingly, this conflicts with Coco Chanel's well-known sentiment that jewelry should be worn to make women feel more beautiful rather than to flaunt one's wealth.

Nevertheless, nearly any authentic piece of Chanel jewelry holds some value on the secondary market, even the most simple in design, and those sold in boutiques today are very pricey. Some styles are more prolific than others, especially with earring designs, but logo enthusiasts will buy it all as long as it is prominently branded as Chanel. This includes tailored gold-tone and pearl

Tweed fabric brooch, c. 2000s, black and white tweed fabric fashioned into a Chanel signature camellia brooch, marked Chanel CC Made in France, 3" wide. **$350-$425**

Jewelry courtesy ChicAntiques.com

Chanel earrings, c. 1997, rhinestone centers set in polished gold-tone rope settings, marked Chanel 97 CC A Made in France, 1" long.
$375-$425

Jewelry courtesy ChicAntiques.com

jewelry from the 1990s that vintage dealers once passed over as undesirable.

There are people who will tell you that all new Chanel jewelry is cheaply made and rather junky in comparison to vintage pieces. While there's no doubt that many pieces marketed by this couturier from the early 2000s through today aren't on par with the older jewelry, there are varying price ranges and quality levels as with many jewelry lines. Some of the couture pieces being made in limited quantities and sold in select Chanel boutiques are quite nicely made, but they definitely don't come cheap. Most of these high-end pieces have a newer feel to them when compared to older Chanel jewelry, but some are indeed top-notch in quality.

If you're going to buy new Chanel at retail, use your discerning collector's eye to select pieces with quality stones, craftsmanship, and materials. Many run-of-the-mill examples don't have the workmanship of the pieces with higher price tags. There's never a guarantee that new jewelry of any type will hold its value, so be sure to buy what you like and enjoy wearing it.

And, of course, one of the most troublesome aspects of collecting jewelry made by the House of Chanel is the proliferation of fakes on the market. There are so many of them out there, many collectors won't risk buying any on the secondary market unless they know the dealer quite well. There's absolutely nothing wrong with this practice; in fact, it's a good idea to turn to someone you trust if you're unsure about what you're doing.

However, there are some basic guidelines about Chanel fakes to keep in mind. First, the quality of the materials used isn't up to par, especially the plating. Authentic Chanel pieces wear much better than fakes plated with far fewer mils of gold or silver. You may see nicks in the plating on items that were mishandled or improperly stored, but you'll rarely see plating worn down to base metal on genuine Chanel.

Earring backs are also a clue. One distinctive style of earring back is most certainly indicative of jewelry that was not made in France for the House of Chanel, although it is marked as such. For more information on identifying fake Chanel earrings, visit the Costume Jewelry Collectors International website at www.cjci.co.

Marks also provide clues to authenticity with this jewelry. With rare exception, jewelry made by the House of Chanel was marked with some type of cartouche or in some cases stamped directly into the metal. The tags can fall off, however, so looking at other components and construction techniques remains imperative before deeming a piece to be a fake. Poorly stamped marks can indeed be indicative of fakes. As a general rule, if a Chanel mark is not clear when you look at it through a jeweler's loupe, that's a red flag. If the piece you're examining screams "fake" in terms of quality, and the mark is also poor, follow your gut instinct and pass on it.

UNDERSTANDING CHANEL MARKS

The earliest Chanel jewelry is unmarked. These pieces, which rarely come on the market now, are identified by the construction and components. From 1954, when the House of Chanel reopened in Paris after World War II, through the 1960s, only a limited number of pieces were marked. One mark used during this time was a round cartouche with CHANEL in block letters with three stars below. Other select pieces are marked simply CHANEL stamped into the metal.

In 1941, Reinad was sued by Chanel (even though Coco had closed her business due to the war) for marking an enameled line of pot metal jewelry with Chanel in script lettering. These pieces have been purported as authentic Chanel in numerous reference guides both in print and online, but later research has shed light on the true origin of these designs as Chanel Novelty Co., which was a division of Reinad.

In the early 1970s, following Coco's death in 1971, Chanel began diligently marking jewelry in various ways:

1. Chanel Made in France

Round metal plaque affixed to metal with copyright and registered symbols, sometimes curved to fit the shape of the piece, used from 1971 through the early 1980s. A similar mark can also be stamped directly into the piece as shown here.

2. Chanel Mid-1980s

Round metal plaque affixed to metal. Mark on pieces dating to the mid-1980s.

3. Chanel Late 1980s through 1992

Oval or round metal plaque with numbers on each side of the CC logo. Number signifies the collection designed by Victoire de Castellane (lead designer for Chanel at the time), in these cases collections 25 and 26. Used from 1986 through the early 1990s.

4. Chanel 1990-2000s

Oval metal plaques of varying sizes depending on the style of each piece. Can also be molded directly into the piece as shown here. First used in 1993 denoting the year made and the season. "P" signifies spring lines; "A," fall lines; "V," summer; and "C," cruise collection pieces. This mark style is still being used on Chanel jewelry, with some oval marks stamped directly into the metal. Most are marked Made in France as part of the signature, but some pieces in the mid-2000s were marked Made in Italy.

Chanel earrings, c. 1980s, glass pearls with matte gold-tone metal findings, marked Chanel 2 CC 8 Made in France, 1 1/2" long. **$275-$325**

Jewelry courtesy ChicAntiques.com

Chanel Gripoix cuff bracelet, c. 1980s, red and green Gripoix glass surrounded by faux pearl accents on a gold-tone base, marked Chanel 2 CC 5 Made in France, 2 1/2" wide at the front. **$6,000-$6,500**

Jewelry courtesy ChicAntiques.com

Madame Coco brooch, c. 1970s, gold-plated Coco Chanel figural brooch with trombone style clasp, marked Chanel CC Made in France, 2 3/8" long. **$275-$325**

Jewelry courtesy ChicAntiques.com

Gripoix necklace, c. 1970s, green and red poured glass with faux pearl accents on Maltese cross as well as the neck chain, marked Chanel CC Made in France. **$3,000-$3,500**

Jewelry courtesy ChicAntiques.com

Chanel brooch, c. 1994, ruby Gripoix glass set in matte-gold-tone CC logo setting with dangling chain tassel, marked Chanel 94 CC A Made in France, 5 3/4" long. **$1,100-$1,200**

Jewelry courtesy ChicAntiques.com

Chanel charm bracelet, c. 1980s, matte gold-tone finish on CC logo charms suspended from matching chain, marked Chanel 2CC8 Made in France, measurements unavailable. **$1,800-$2,000**

Jewelry courtesy ChicAntiques.com

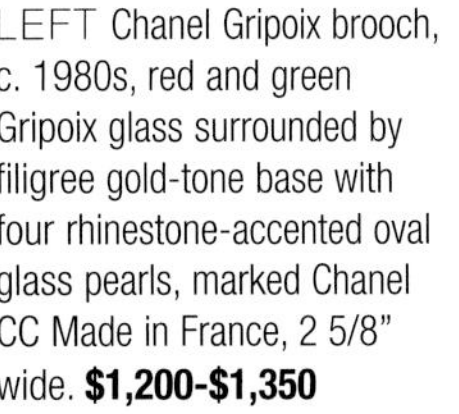

LEFT Chanel Gripoix brooch, c. 1980s, red and green Gripoix glass surrounded by filigree gold-tone base with four rhinestone-accented oval glass pearls, marked Chanel CC Made in France, 2 5/8" wide. **$1,200-$1,350**

Jewelry courtesy ChicAntiques.com

ABOVE Chanel Gripoix earrings, c. 1980s, pearl drop encased with matte gold-tone metal and square Gripoix pearls at the top, marked Chanel CC Made in France, 2 3/4" long. **$650-$800**

Jewelry courtesy ChicAntiques.com

CINER

DESIGNERS AND MANUFACTURERS

If your taste leans toward classic and you value quality, Ciner jewelry will offer just what you're seeking. One thing to keep in mind about the jewelry made and sold by Ciner is that the company has been producing some of the same designs for decades. A visit to its New York showroom is an eye-popping experience, in fact, because as you peruse the trays of samples available to wholesale buyers, there are many 1950s and 1960s pieces mixed in with the company's contemporary designs.

Another aspect gleaned from a Ciner showroom experience, and one that many collectors aren't aware of, revolves around pricing. Many of the prices for Ciner jewelry are much lower on the secondary market than the wholesale prices being charged by the company today. Yes, what retailers pay to carry Ciner in their stores is higher than what collectors pay for vintage to newer Ciner, making this jewelry a real steal in the secondary marketplace.

The earliest Ciner costume jewelry manufactured during the 1930s in the fine jewelry tradition was actually made in sterling silver long before other companies began using this metal due to World War II rationing. These pieces are hard to come by today. There is stiff competition to snag them among Art Deco collectors, too, so plan to pay good sums if you can locate a piece in pristine condition. Ciner hasn't worked in sterling since those early days, so it's easier to date these pieces than other adornments fashioned by this company.

Ciner used many different marks over its history, and reused them through the decades, so it's all but impossible to circa date solely by the way a piece is signed. The plating finishes have changed a bit over the years and some of the newer stones used in classic designs are slightly different when comparing new to old. To get serious about dating this type of jewelry, visit retailers carrying current Ciner lines to learn what to look for in new pieces.

This company's animal cuff bracelets and matching necklaces are perennial favorites, as are its phenomenal jeweled earrings. Keep in mind, however, that many pieces being sold as vintage are new production, and the folks doing the selling don't usually know the difference. Ciner jewelry is collectible as a whole, though, so buying what you like is a good guide. New or old, it's still quality jewelry with style to spare regardless of the age.

Ciner necklace, c. 2000s, variation of a classic Ciner style using high quality imitation baroque pearls and gray rhinestone rondelles, marked Ciner, 17" long. **$325-$400**

Jewelry courtesy ChicAntiques.com

Ciner mogul style brooch, c. 2000s, variation of a classic Ciner design made in the 1960s using jewel tones of emerald green, sapphire blue, and ruby red, marked Ciner. **$250-$325**

Jewelry courtesy ChicAntiques.com

Ciner brooch, c. 1990s, central simulated pearl surrounded by clear rhinestones with brown and black enameling, marked Ciner, 2 1/2" centerpiece. **$225-$275**

Jewelry courtesy ChicAntiques.com

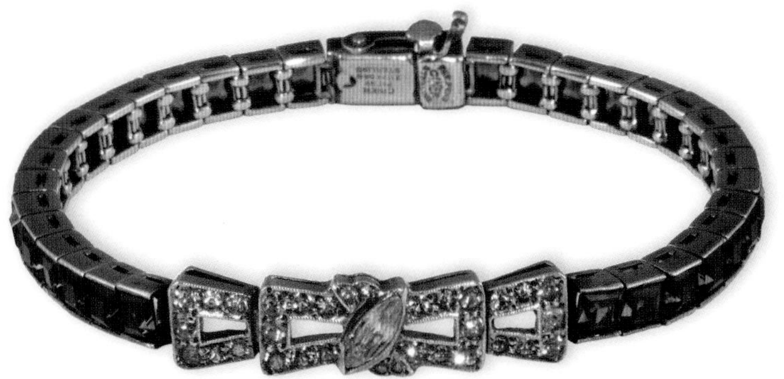

Ciner bracelet, c. 1937, sterling silver articulated line bracelet set with unfoiled square-cut simulated sapphires set open backed with an articulated central rhinestone-embellished element with a bow motif, marked CINER PAT NO 2074046 STERLING, 7" long. **$475-$675**

Jewelry courtesy Robin Deutsch Collection

Ciner Hinged Cuff Bracelet c.1937

This phenomenal Ciner hinged cuff bracelet was featured in a January 1938 *Life Magazine* article on "Junk Jewelry." It was the most expensive piece illustrated at $100. This rarely found example of Ciner's early work is solid sterling silver in graduated style that clasps with a hidden hook in the front. It features alternating rows of channel-set calibré-cut faux sapphires and pavé bead-set round rhinestones. Every stone is set open backed. The exquisite workmanship of this piece reflects Ciner's origin as a fine jewelry company that began replicating jewelry models previously made of precious metal and gemstones in sterling silver and rhinestones in the early 1930s. Marked CINER STERLING in block letters in two places, 50.7 grams, 2 3/4" at the widest point on the top graduating to 1/2" on the bottom. It's interesting to note that a ring matching this piece was featured in a 1939 Saks Fifth Avenue Christmas advertisement. **$2,500-$2,750**

Jewelry courtesy Robin Deutsch Collection

Ciner earrings, c. early 1960s, round and navette clear rhinestones in a leaf motif with dangling pearls beneath, marked Ciner, 1 3/4" long. **$125-$150**

Jewelry courtesy LinsyJsJewels.com

Ciner sterling ring, c. 1937-1939, set with two French-cut faux sapphires bordered by a single row of pavé-set round rhinestones, top width approximately 1/2". **$450-$550**

Jewelry courtesy Robin Deutsch Collection

Ciner earrings, c. late 1950s, round and baguette clear rhinestones in a knotted design with three independently dangling elements terminating in pear-shaped stones on each earring, marked Ciner, 3 1/8" long. **$225-$275**

Jewelry courtesy LinsyJsJewels.com

Ciner double clip brooch, c.1936, rare, all stones are set open backed, detaches into two separate dress clips that can be rejoined onto the sterling frame to be worn as a brooch; each clip has bead-, bezel-, and prong-set silver foiled pastes punctuated by a large emerald-cut faceted unfoiled glass simulated sapphire and bullet-nosed cabochons on either side in a millegrain mounting; each clip is marked CINER STERLING; as a brooch, 3" long x 1 1/2", 43.9 grams. **$1,500-$1,750**

Jewelry courtesy the Robin Deutsch Collection

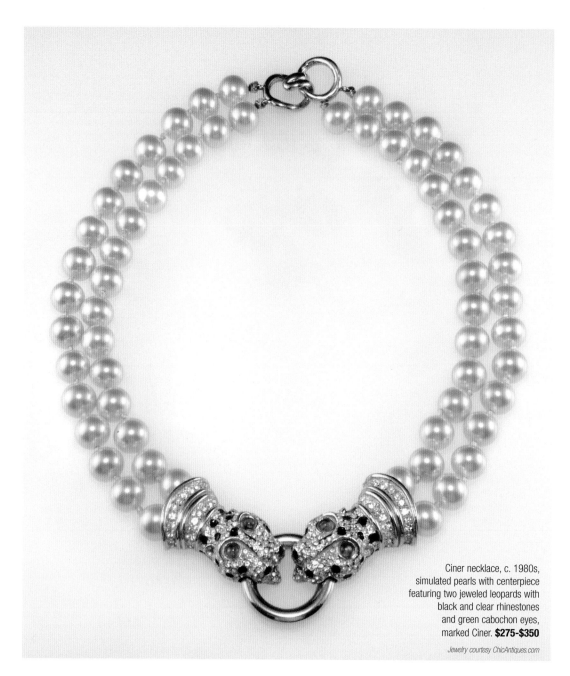

Ciner necklace, c. 1980s, simulated pearls with centerpiece featuring two jeweled leopards with black and clear rhinestones and green cabochon eyes, marked Ciner. **$275-$350**

Jewelry courtesy ChicAntiques.com

RIGHT Ciner flower brooch, c. 2000s, gold-tone metal with simulated pearls and clear rhinestones, marked Ciner. **$225-$275**

Jewelry courtesy ChicAntiques.com

FAR RIGHT Ciner sterling Art Deco swirl dress clip, c. 1937, comprised of navette, baguette, and round rhinestones set in a three-dimensional scrolled millegrain setting, all stones are set open back, dress clip fastening mechanism, marked CINER STERLING. **$275-$375**

Jewelry courtesy Robin Deutsch Collection

Ciner earrings, c. 1980s, simulated coral centers surrounded by black glass ovals and clear rhinestone accents, marked Ciner. **$125-$150**

Jewelry courtesy ChicAntiques.com

Ciner pendant necklace, c. 2000s, black glass beads with imitation pearls and black rhinestones embellishing the pendant, marked Ciner, 17" long with 3" centerpiece. **$275-$350**

Jewelry courtesy ChicAntiques.com

CORO & VENDÔME

DESIGNERS AND MANUFACTURERS

Coro, founded as Cohn and Rosenberger in the early 1900s, was the most prolific manufacturer of costume jewelry in American history. This company literally turned out millions of pieces of jewelry in various levels of quality ranging from dime store trinkets to high dollar sterling figurals. And it marketed jewelry under many different brands. Among the most well known are Coro, of course, along with Corocraft and Vendôme.

Some Corocraft pieces were also marked sterling within the signature plaque. Other sterling pieces were made with the simple Coro mark and separately marked as such. There are literally dozens of other marks used on brands conceived and marketed by Coro, including Francois and Glamour. A more detailed list is available through the Researching Costume Jewelry Marks information for Coro provided by IllusionJewels.com.

The truth about the most commonly found Coro pieces is that they are of the lower-end variety made during the 1950s and 1960s. These were sold by the boatload when they were new, and they aren't highly valuable in today's secondary marketplace. The styles are often simple and the materials and construction indicative of their affordable beginnings. They're nice to wear, no doubt, but not highly desirable as collectibles.

On the other hand, there are some magnificent Coro and Corocraft pieces produced in the 1930s and 1940s that collectors will pay dearly to own. These include exquisite figurals, a variety of jelly bellies (see Trifari

for more information on this type of jewelry), and Coro's famed Duette clips.

The first branded Duettes by Coro were Art Deco styles patented in 1931. These clever mechanisms held two dress clips in place to make a brooch, or could be removed to wear clipped to the corners of a square neckline or a jacket pocket. Other companies made their versions of this style of clip/brooch mechanism, and they can also be found unmarked. Collectors have adopted the generic name "duette" when referencing this type of jewelry. Coro later made Duettes with small double-pronged clips (also known by collectors as "fur clips"), especially in the 1940s; most of these were figural clips shaped like horse heads, bees, and the like.

Vendôme brooch, c. 1950s, purple inverted rhinestones and simulated pearls surrounded by aurora borealis stones in rhodium-plated setting, marked Vendôme, 2 3/4" wide. **$135-$165**

Courtesy of ChicAntiques.com

Many of Coro's most desirable pieces were designed by Gene Verri, although Adolph Katz submitted the majority of the paperwork for these designs to the patent office as a Coro executive. Nevertheless, the Internet is riddled with references attributing Katz as a Coro designer for this firm, which is untrue based on past interviews conducted with both Gene Verri and his son, Ron. Katz misattributed as a designer is an understandable deduction based on patent research, but erroneous nonetheless. Verri's designs are revered by collectors as some of the finest produced during costume jewelry's "golden age." This design master, also noted for being very gentlemanly by jewelry historian Robin Deutsch, passed away in early 2013. Ron Verri continues to operate the Rhode Island jewelry company Gem-Craft, which was founded by Gene and Alfeo Verri.

The mark Vendôme was used by Coro beginning in 1944, but it is most noted on finely crafted beaded jewelry made during the 1950s and 1960s. A fleur de lis symbol often graces the tail of the closure on bead necklaces. This brand was one of several to use a screw-clip mechanism that allows the tension of earrings to be adjusted for comfort. Rhinestone jewelry marked Vendôme is harder to come by than the beaded pieces, and also of high quality.

Vendôme bracelet, c. late 1950s, iridescent cabochons surrounded by yellow and blue aurora borealis rhinestones in a silver-tone setting, marked Vendôme, 7 1/4" long x 1 1/4" wide. **$150-$200**

Author's Collection

Vendôme necklace, c. late 1950s, dangling iridescent crystal necklace with clear rhinestone accents, marked Vendôme, 16 1/2" long. **$125-$150**

Courtesy of ChicAntiques.com

Vendôme necklace, c. early 1960s, bright pink rhinestones with aurora borealis in rhodium-plated setting, marked Vendôme, necklace adjusts from about 16 1/4" to 17" long. **$150-$175**

Courtesy of ChicAntiques.com

Vendôme earrings, c. late 1950s, pink cabochons and aurora borealis accents with screw clip backs, marked Vendôme. **$65-$85**

Courtesy of ChicAntiques.com

Coro brooch, c. late 1940s, gold-plated bow with purple rhinestone embellishments and clear accents, 2 1/2" wide, marked Coro. **$100-$150**

Jewelry courtesy ChicAntiques.com

Vendôme brooch, c. 1950s, purple and blue bicolor faceted beads and rhinestone accents mounted on silver-tone filigree backing, marked Vendôme, 2" wide. **$100-$135**

Courtesy of ChicAntiques.com

Coro Duette set, c. 1948, swirled green and clear rhinestone Duette with matching earrings, worn together as brooch or separately as two pin clips, brooch marked Coro Duette on the frame, earrings marked Coro. **$150-$200**

Jewelry courtesy ChicAntiques.com

Coro October Angels Duette, c. 1956, matte gold-tone angel pin clips joined together by patented Duette mechanism, one angel holds October star and other holds heart-shaped pink October birthstone, marked Coro Duette on the frame, 2 1/2" wide. **$125-$200**

Jewelry courtesy ChicAntiques.com

Coro horse head Duette, c. late 1940s, red, green and clear rhinestones, can be worn as a brooch as shown or separate into two pin clips, marked Corocraft on each horse and Coro Duette on the frame, 2 1/2" wide. **$275-$375**

Jewelry courtesy ChicAntiques.com

LEFT Coro Siempre Amigos brooch, c. 1942, enameled brooch with 21 flags represented at the 1938 Friendship Conference of North and South America held in Lima, Peru; the brooch was produced to raise money for the Inter-American Scholarship Fund; marked Coro, 2 3/4" long. **$125-$175**

Jewelry courtesy ChicAntiques.com

BELOW Corocraft brooch, c. 1948, patented design featuring jewel-embellished donkey pulling a rhinestone-embellished flower cart, marked Corocraft, 2 1/4" long. **$125-$175**

Jewelry courtesy ChicAntiques.com

Vendôme Victorian revival necklace, c. 1960s, black glass domed components with black crystals and seed beads simulating jet in mourning jewelry style with Vendôme signature fleur de lis dangling from the closure tail, marked Vendôme, adjusts to 16 1/2" long, longest dangle is 3 1/4". **$275-$375**

Courtesy of ChicAntiques.com

DELIZZA & ELSTER'S "JULIANA"

DESIGNERS AND MANUFACTURERS

While the styles we now know as "Juliana" were made from the late 1950s through the 1980s, it's important to note that DeLizza & Elster only marked them with paper hangtags when they were new and only for a short time. The tags identifying early pieces were largely discarded when the jewelry was worn by the original owners, leaving the pieces unsigned today. It's also interesting how recognizing pieces as Juliana came about, and it all started with the familiar link and band bracelets.

The Juliana journey was actually a marvel to witness. In the mid-2000s, collectors participating in an online listserv remarked how pieces of jewelry that matched bracelets with a five link and band construction were being discovered from time to time with paper hangtags that read "Juliana Original." The Juliana nickname for this type of jewelry stuck, and is still being used today.

But as the pieces that matched those ubiquitous Juliana bracelets were examined more closely, common construction techniques and stones used in the designs were identified. In fact, the author of this book pointed out that a particular type of heavy rivet sparingly used in many of these pieces was different from those used by most other manufacturers. Not long after, Cheryl Kilmer of Chicago, a long-time collector of this style of jewelry, made contact with Frank DeLizza, many pieces of this jewelry were identified as Delizza & Elster, and a mystery was truly solved.

DeLizza & Elster bracelet, c. 1960s, cat's eye cabochons with red and gray rhinestones in silver-tone metal, 7 1/4" long. **$225-$275**

Jewelry courtesy ChicAntiques.com

ABOVE DeLizza & Elster parure, c. 1960s, considered rare (only 100 or so were made, per Frank DeLizza), pink matrix cabochons with fuchsia, red, and aurora borealis rhinestones, necklace 15" long x 2" wide, brooch 3 3/4" long, earrings 1" long. **$1,400-$1,500**

Author's Collection

LEFT DeLizza & Elster bracelet, c. 1960s, pink molded glass leaf stones with pink and aurora borealis rhinestones in gold-tone setting, 7 1/2" long. **$165-$195**

Jewelry courtesy ChicAntiques.com

DeLizza & Elster brooch, c. 1960s, margarita bicolor, "watermelon," and vivid rivolis with red and purple rhinestones in gold-tone metal, 2 3/4" wide. **$200-$250**

Jewelry courtesy ChicAntiques.com

As more people have learned to recognize Juliana jewelry, the market has become flooded with the more ordinary pieces. These still sell, but only if priced very reasonably. They're great for beginning collectors or folks who just want something sparkly to wear at a budget-minded price point. The magnificent sets and grand parures in vibrant colors with artsy stones such as rivolis, margaritas, and stippled cabochons still bring good prices, and values are holding steady for the truly rare and most popular examples.

That's not to say that there aren't pieces of jewelry on the market nowadays that are purported to be Juliana that don't measure up to this company's work. That's where all the identification resources, including those provided in Section Three of this reference, come in handy for collectors. Even though these pieces are unmarked, you can learn to recognize telltale signs of their origin. And as more and more styles are confirmed and documented as true DeLizza & Elster products, they are also listed in online resources and in reference guides on the topic.

DeLizza & Elster made jewelry for brands such as Hattie Carnegie, Kenneth Jay Lane, and Weiss, along with many other familiar companies. If you find pieces marked with these brands and they look like known Juliana pieces, it's likely this manufacturer produced them.

As a side note, it has been reported that Frank DeLizza frowns upon collectors using the Juliana name in reference to all jewelry made by DeLizza & Elster. But when asked about this in a face-to-face conversation with the author of this book, he rather humbly invoked Shakespeare and replied, "A rose by any other name…" He very gentlemanly alluded to the admiration for his company's baubles by collectors as being much appreciated, and left it at that.

See more examples of DeLizza & Elster jewelry, including back views, in Section Three.

RIGHT DeLizza & Elster set, c. 1960s, red and black art glass dangle drops with black beads and red, black and clear rhinestones, brooch 3 1/4" long, earrings 1 1/8" diameter. **$275-$325**

Jewelry courtesy ChicAntiques.com

FAR RIGHT DeLizza & Elster set, c. 1960s, pink "Italian marble" cabochons with aurora borealis rhinestones and leafy findings in gold-tone setting, brooch 2 1/4" diameter, earrings 2" long. **$195-$225**

Jewelry courtesy ChicAntiques.com

DeLizza & Elster "carved" glass parure, c. 1960s, blue molded glass ovals (often described as "carved" by collectors) with tiny fuchsia accent stones amid rhinestones of varying shades of blue, necklace 16" long, bracelet 7 1/4" long, earrings 1 1/4" long. **$475-$575**

Jewelry courtesy ChicAntiques.com

DeLizza & Elster bracelet, c. 1960s, opaque blue copper swirl pear-shaped stones with sapphire blue rhinestones in gold-tone setting, missing safety chain, 7" long. **$195-$225**

Jewelry courtesy ChicAntiques.com

DeLizza & Elster pressed glass parure, c. 1960s, blue molded glass ovals with floral pattern and blue aurora borealis accents in gold-tone settings, necklace 17" long, bracelet 7", earrings 1 1/4" long. **$350-$400**

Jewelry courtesy ChicAntiques.com

DeLizza & Elster parure, c. 1960s, unfoiled blue oversized navettes with blue rhinestones and aurora borealis accents in gold-tone setting, necklace 15 1/2" long x 1 5/8" wide at the center, brooch 2" wide, earrings 1 1/2" long. **$275-$300**

Jewelry courtesy ChicAntiques.com

DeLizza & Elster parure, c. 1960s, foiled bead and iridescent dangles with aurora borealis and gray unfoiled rhinestones, necklace 16" long with 3 1/2" drop at the front, brooch 2 1/4" wide, bracelet 7" long x 1 1/4" wide, earrings 1 1/2" long. **$1,100-$1,300**

Author's Collection

DIOR

DESIGNERS AND MANUFACTURERS

The House of Dior jewelry most often sought by collectors exudes glamour and femininity, just as Christian Dior's "New Look" fashions did when they were introduced in 1947. The couturier founded Masion Dior in Paris in 1945, and his work called for beautiful jewelry to accentuate the lines of the garments he designed. Of course, he was no newcomer to the industry, having previously worked alongside Pierre Balmain as a fellow designer for famed Parisian couturier Lucien Lelong.

Many collectors, however, don't realize that most of the costume jewelry pieces they seek were made after Christian Dior's sudden death of a heart attack in 1957. In fact, Henkel and Grosse began adding dates to the signature plaques of Dior pieces made in the German factory from then on. After Dior's passing, Yves Saint Laurent took the helm, continuing a legacy of designing exquisite clothing and accessories. Henkel and Grosse held the license to produce Dior jewelry through 1980.

Some earlier Dior pieces were designed by Josette Gripoix, and like jewelry from the House of Chanel during the same period, these include the magnificent glass components for which the House of Gripoix is known. Other pieces made between 1952 and 1955 (some sources cite 1956) were designed by Mitchel Maer of London, and they are marked indicating the affiliation. Pieces made for Dior by Kramer in the 1950s are also marked as such.

The tradition of adding dates to Dior jewelry continued through the 1970s, which is fortuitous for collectors. In examining Dior pieces, some that look as if they were made much later are dated in the 1950s and early 1960s, and some dating to the 1970s look much more like 1950s designs using brilliantly colored rhinestones and richly hued cabochons to create pieces worthy of their haute couture origin.

The pieces that were still being made by Henkel and Grosse in Germany in the late 1970s are signed with an Art Deco-style marquee emblem similar to that used earlier in the decade, but without the date. Styles indicative of the 1980s can be found with oval plaques spelling out Christian Dior. Newer pieces are marked simply Chr. Dior. All Dior jewelry is high quality, even demure styles made in the early 1990s. The newer pieces can, of course, be collected more affordably than the older, rarer designs.

ABOVE Dior necklace, c. 1974, Art Deco-inspired design featuring black resin, brushed gold-tone metal links and pavé-set rhinestone accents, marked 1974 Chr. Dior Germany, 19 1/4" long. **$125-$175**

Author's Collection

RIGHT Dior brooch, c. 1961, large square clear unfoiled stones with round gray rhinestones, marked 1961 Chr. Dior, 4 1/4" long. **$325-$400**

Author's Collection

Dior brooch, c. 1968, domed brooch with jade green cabochons and clear rhinestones, marked Chr. Dior Germany 1968, 2 1/4" long. **$225-$300**

Author's Collection

Dior monogram brooch, c. late 1970s, C. Dior spelled out in clear rhinestones, rhodium-plated setting, marked Chr. Dior © and Germany, 2" wide. **$125-$175**

Author's Collection

Dior heart necklace, c. 1973, black and frosted resin with rhinestone rondelles and silver-tone beads, marked 1973 Chr. Dior Germany, 16 1/2" long.
$175-$225

Jewelry courtesy ChicAntiques.com

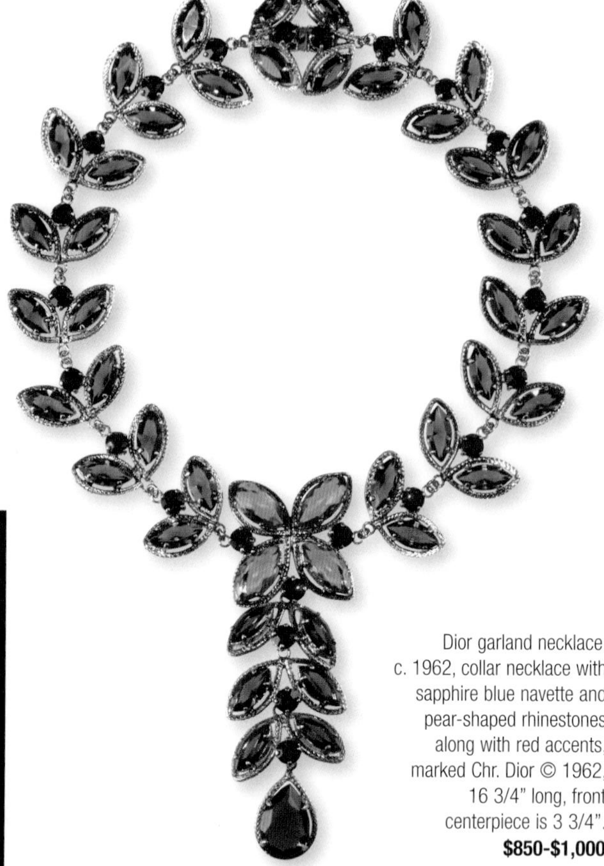

Dior garland necklace, c. 1962, collar necklace with sapphire blue navette and pear-shaped rhinestones along with red accents, marked Chr. Dior © 1962, 16 3/4" long, front centerpiece is 3 3/4".
$850-$1,000

Author's Collection

Dior Edwardian revival necklace, c. 2000s, comprised of high quality glass pearls and pavé-set rhinestone accents, marked Dior, adjusts to 16 1/2" long.
$275-$325

Author's Collection

Dior brooch, c. 1962, domed brooch with red, clear, and blue rhinestones along with faux pearls and coordinating glass beads, marked Made in Germany for Christian Dior 1962, 3 5/8" long. **$550-$700**

Author's Collection

Dior domed brooch, c. 1962, impressive, set with red, clear, and blue rhinestones, faux pearls, and coordinating glass beads, marked Made in Germany for Christian Dior 1962, 2 3/8" wide. **$650-$775**

Author's Collection

Dior necklace, c. 1970, faux ruby cabochons with clear round and navette rhinestones, marked 1970 Chr. Dior Germany, 18 3/4" long, domed center section is 2 3/4" long. **$650-$700**

Author's Collection

Dior by Mitchell Maer parure, c. mid-1950s, circles of clear rhinestones joined by links of emerald-cut sapphire blue stones, marked Mitchell Maer for Dior, necklace 16" long, brooch 2 1/8" wide, earrings 1 1/4" long. **$1,200-$1,500**

Jewelry courtesy LinsyJsJewels.com

EISENBERG

DESIGNERS AND MANUFACTURERS

The well-known story of Eisenberg & Sons began in Chicago in the mid-1930s. To enhance frocks being sold in its dress shops, the company added sparkling rhinestone clips and brooches to the garments, and soon they began to disappear. Demand for the baubles exceeded that of the clothing, and eventually jewelry became the sole focus of the enterprise.

The early, and rare, Eisenberg jewelry sought by collectors today was made by Fallon & Kappel in New York. Ruth Kamke, who designed a majority of the rarities as an employee of the company, found inspiration for jewelry designs at every turn. Whether it was a visit to a museum, interesting stones presented to her, or a crude sketch of another that sparked creativity, her work is considered genius today and collectors pay dearly to own it.

While Kamke's designs were purchased by other famous couture clients like Hattie Carnegie early on, Fallon & Kappel is said to have eventually signed an exclusive agreement to only produce jewelry for Eisenberg if Eisenberg would only purchase product from Fallon & Kappel's factory. This agreement supposedly stood until 1972 when Fallon & Kappel closed, according to some sources. However, former employees of at least one Rhode Island manufacturer have gone on record stating that Eisenberg jewelry was made

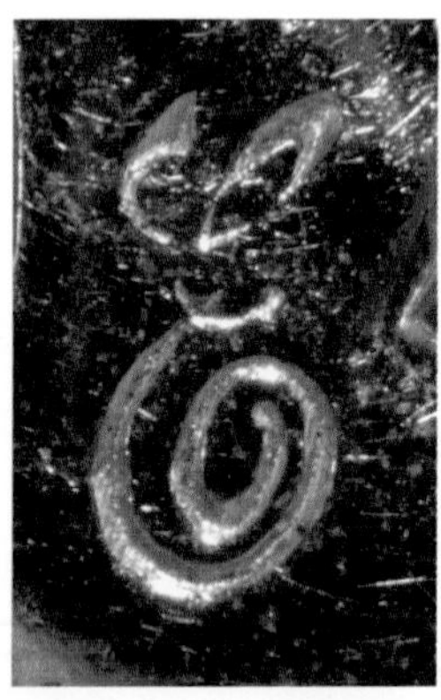

alongside similar Weiss pieces in the 1950s, and the same jewelry designs stamped with each mark independently serve as evidence.

Regardless of the source of Eisenberg jewelry, the company's owners made sure the product bearing the Eisenberg name was always of high quality and intriguing in one way or another. The early Kamke designs Eisenberg selected for production, many of which were made in low quantities with a minimum of 144, ranged from Art Deco-influenced clips to fanciful brooches depicting mermaids, Puss 'n Boots, and other whimsical figural shapes. Eisenberg jewelry, regardless of when it was made, mesmerized consumers with dazzling Swarovski crystals in highly faceted varieties.

Marks used by Eisenberg varied over time, and early pieces were signed in a variety of ways. Eisenberg Original was used on jewelry from 1935-1945, but the company also used script and block "E" marks in the 1940s. Pieces from the 1950s have been found marked Eisenberg in block capital letters. Later jewelry made in the 1970s through the 1990s, including colorful Christmas pins, were often marked Eisenberg Ice, although some unsigned jewelry was marketed during this period as well. The Eisenberg Ice tagline in advertising was used much earlier in the company's history, even in the late 1930s.

Anomalies also occurred where pieces with clear 1940s characteristics were only marked Eisenberg in block letters, indicating an overlap in marks as far as dating is concerned. Companies like this had no clue that collectors would be trying to pinpoint the date their jewelry was manufactured 50, 60, or 70 years after it was made, so using marks for this purpose isn't always precise. Learning to identify attributes from different eras as they relate to specific companies is paramount to avoid making mistakes in this area.

ABOVE Eisenberg Original fur clip, c. late 1930s, red and pink rhinestones with simulated pearls in heavy cast setting, marked Eisenberg Original, 3 1/2" long. **$625-$750**

Jewelry courtesy LinsyJsJewels.com

BELOW Eisenberg Original fur clip, c. 1940s, sterling set with sapphire blue rhinestones and clear accents, marked Eisenberg Original, 2 1/2" long. **$650-$800**

Jewelry courtesy LinsyJsJewels.com

RIGHT Eisenberg Original fur clips, c. 1935, pair of clips set with cranberry red rhinestones and clear accents, marked Eisenberg Original, each clip is 1 3/4" long. **$450-600**

Jewelry courtesy LinsyJsJewels.com

LEFT Eisenberg Original clip in box, c. 1930s, classic styling with a variety of clear rhinestones including large emerald-cut stones, marked Eisenberg Original, 2 5/8" long. **$250-$300**

Jewelry courtesy ChicAntiques.com

Eisenberg ring in box, c. early 1940s, large clear emerald-cut rhinestone with side accents set in silver-tone metal, adjustable sizing, marked Eisenberg. **$225-$275**

Jewelry courtesy ChicAntiques.com

Eisenberg Original fur clip, c. late 1930s, leaf motif with green enameling and clear rhinestones set in pot metal, marked Eisenberg Original, 3 1/2" wide. **$550-$700**

Jewelry courtesy LinsyJsJewels.com

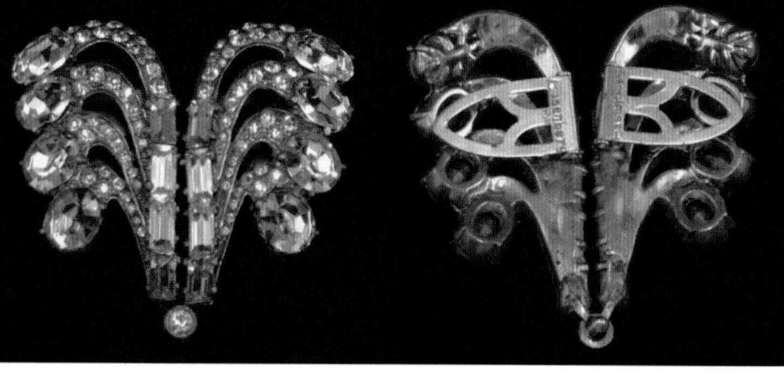

ABOVE Eisenberg adjustable clip, c. 1930s, unusual double dress clip that can be adjusted to wear a variety of ways, clear rhinestones set in pot metal, marked Eisenberg on each clip back. **$350-$400**

Jewelry courtesy ChicAntiques.com

BELOW Eisenberg Original brooch, c. early 1940s, considered rare, large eagle set with clear rhinestones and black enamel on feet, marked Eisenberg Original, 3 3/4" wide. **$1,100-$1,500**

Jewelry courtesy LinsyJsJewels.com

Eisenberg Original fur clip, c. 1940, glass opalescent blue stones with simulated sapphire bullet cabochon accents and clear rhinestones with simulated pearls in heavy cast setting, marked Eisenberg Original, 4" long. **$1,100-$1,300**

Jewelry courtesy LinsyJsJewels.com

Eisenberg Original bracelet, c. 1940s, large emerald-cut rhinestones with smaller accents set in sterling silver, marked Eisenberg Original, 8 1/2" long x 3/4" wide. **$425-$550**

Jewelry courtesy LinsyJsJewels.com

Eisenberg Original brooch, c. 1940s, purple and clear rhinestones set in sterling silver, marked Eisenberg Original, 3 1/4" long. **$725-$900**

Jewelry courtesy LinsyJsJewels.com

Eisenberg brooch, c. 1940s, Maltese cross motif in enameled sterling silver set with red and clear rhinestones, marked "E" script mark, 1 3/4" long. **$300-$450**

Jewelry courtesy LinsyJsJewels.com

Eisenberg Original fur clip, c. 1940s, amber specialty stones with rhinestone accents set in sterling silver with gold wash, marked Eisenberg Original, 3 1/4" long. **$450-600**

Jewelry courtesy LinsyJsJewels.com

Is it Eisenberg?

Along with pieces made bearing the Weiss, Hobé, and K.J.L. marks, many pieces of low- to mid-end costume jewelry made in the early 2000s bearing the Eisenberg Ice name are designs that were never originally sold by this company. They aren't technically reproductions, but rather fantasy pieces also known as counterfeits because they aren't duplicates of designs ever marketed by Eisenberg.

The butterfly shown here is one of these "fantasy" pieces never marketed by this company but marked Eisenberg Ice on a plaque identical to legitimate tags used from the 1970s on. It is beautiful costume jewelry, large in size at 3 1/2" wide, and well constructed with quality stones, but it is not genuine Eisenberg as confirmed by the company at the time they were made.

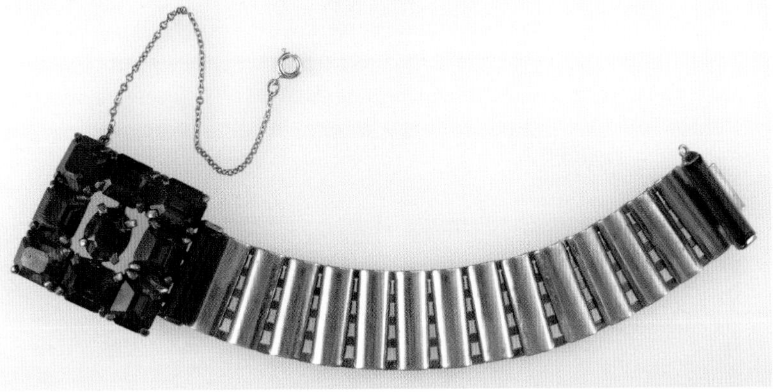

ABOVE Eisenberg parure, c. 1950s, bright green and pale yellow rhinestones in gold-tone setting, each piece is marked Eisenberg, necklace adjusts to 17" long, bracelet is 6 3/4"; earrings are 1" long. **$550-$700**

Jewelry courtesy LinsyJsJewels.com

LEFT Eisenberg Original bracelet, c. late 1930s, cranberry red rhinestones decorate the clasp with hidden closure, marked Eisenberg Original, 7" long with 1 3/8" clasp. **$850-$1,000**

Jewelry courtesy LinsyJsJewels.com

HASKELL

DESIGNERS AND MANUFACTURERS

Miriam Haskell jewelry remains a perennial favorite among collectors. Its popularity wanes slightly, and before you know it everyone starts asking for "Haskell" again. This style of hand-manipulated jewelry, made with baroque pearls, beads of varying sizes, rose montee rhinestones, and glass elements wired to antiqued gold-tone filigree backings, intrigues those driven to own it. These are the most popular of the Haskell designs made by the company under every designer employed, from Frank Hess to current production.

But there are other Haskell styles that also have a following with collectors, including the innovations brought about by Lawrence Vrba in the 1970s. Vrba was responsible for the company's widely acclaimed Egyptian revival line and other jewelry that completely broke away from the "same old Haskell" to incorporate modern colors and new, unique designs customers were clamoring to own. Many of these pieces share some traditional Haskell elements, but they often surprise collectors when they discover the Haskell signature upon further examination.

Miriam Haskell jewelry was marked in several different ways, and most of it made since the late 1940s has been signed. But unlike many other costume jewelry companies, you can't date Haskell jewelry solely by the signature. There are a few exceptions, including the earliest marked pieces made after World War II. These have a horseshoe-shaped mark that is very distinctive. Be aware, however, that some people incorrectly attribute this signature to Haskell's earliest jewelry made in the 1920s and 1930s, rather than Haskell's earliest *marked* jewelry.

Another distinctive characteristic is a small rectangular "paperclip" clasp that was first used in the 1970s. If you see a piece with this type of clasp, you'll know it dates to the 1970s or later. Some pieces made during the era of this clasp reincarnate the book chain-style necklace popular in the Victorian era and again in the 1920s and 1930s, to which various beads and dangles were added. Regardless of the styling of the piece, if it has a rectangular clasp, it's not early Haskell.

Early Haskell pieces made from 1926 until after World War II were not marked at all. Many of them do have distinctive characteristics that aid in identification, however,

and a number of these are shown in Section Three of this book. In fact, once you learn to recognize unmarked Haskell jewelry, it's sometimes easier to date than pieces with the more common oval mark first employed in the late 1940s and still used today.

Using findings (the component parts or materials used in making a piece of jewelry) and overall styles isn't a foolproof indicator of age with this jewelry either. Many of the same hooks, clasps, bead caps, and other components have been used on Haskell pieces through the company's history, even still today, so keep this in mind.

Among the makers of this type of hand-manipulated jewelry – and there were many companies that made similar styles – Haskell is by and large the finest. Nevertheless, the wiring used on older pieces is prone to corrosion, and the deteriorating metal can cause damage to pearl components. Only Haskell pieces in excellent condition should command the highest prices.

It's also wise to remember that shady characters have been known to change out clasps to make unsigned non-Haskell pieces more valuable. Other crooks have reworked Haskell pieces using original components, sometimes mixing them with new beads and findings, and then passed them off to unsuspecting customers as originals.

ABOVE Miriam Haskell brooch, c. late-1950s, light green glass leaves and white iridescent elements with rose montee aurora borealis rhinestones, marked Miriam Haskell, 2 7/8" wide. **$325-$475**

Jewelry courtesy LinsyJsJewels.com

LEFT Miriam Haskell brooch set, c. late 1940s, floral motif with large blue glass stones surrounded by clear faceted and rose montee rhinestones, marked Miriam Haskell horseshoe mark, brooch 2 1/4" wide, earrings 1". **$500-675**

Jewelry courtesy LinsyJsJewels.com

GEMSCOPE
an in-depth look

Is it authentic Haskell?

Many pieces of Miriam Haskell jewelry look beautiful at first glance, as shown in the front view of the necklace here. The components appear to be original and in very nice condition. But when the back is examined, there's evidence that the piece is not of original construction.

The most obvious evidence this necklace is not "right" is wiring across the signature plaque on the back of the piece. Then you have the silver-colored wire wrapped around the brass leaves along the edges, which presents a couple of problems. First, the wire in an original piece of this nature would be brass-tone to match the other findings. And even more important, original pieces are finished on the back so that messy wiring like this is not evident. A necklace or any other jewelry would never leave the Haskell factory looking like this.

Upon closer inspection of the components, you also notice that the tiny brass spacers between the baroque pearls are not the shape that Haskell would have used on a piece of this nature, and they look too new under magnification. The rose montee rhinestones embellishing the florets are also new.

These are just a few of the attributes of reassembled jewelry that may be represented as original Haskell by unknowing or unscrupulous sellers. Learn the attributes of genuine vintage Haskell to avoid making very costly mistakes purchasing pieces like these.

Miriam Haskell pastel necklace, c. 1950s, pastel beads and rhinestones with silver simulated baroque pearls, marked Miriam Haskell, necklace 15" long with 3 1/4" centerpiece. **$375-$425**

Jewelry courtesy ChicAntiques.com

Miriam Haskell sweater guard, c. late 1940s, unusual style featuring pink glass flowers with bead and rhinestone accents, marked Miriam Haskell horseshoe mark, 3 1/4" wide. **$325-$450**

Jewelry courtesy LinsyJsJewels.com

Miriam Haskell brooch, c. 1950s, antiqued gold-tone chain fashioned into bow shape with floral findings, simulated pearls and rhinestone embellishments, marked Miriam Haskell, 5" long x 3 1/8". **$275-$350**

Jewelry courtesy ChicAntiques.com

Miriam Haskell brooch set, c. 1950s, red, blue, and clear mirror cabochons with turquoise blue bead and clear rose montee rhinestone accents, marked Miriam Haskell, brooch 3 1/2" wide, earrings 1 1/8". **$650-$775**

Jewelry courtesy LinsyJsJewels.com

BELOW Miriam Haskell oval pearls, c. 1960s, a different twist on classic Haskell baroque glass pearls in oval shapes with flat backs so they lay flat on the neckline, marked Miriam Haskell, necklace 16 1/2" long. **$175-$225**

Jewelry courtesy ChicAntiques.com

Miriam Haskell Pearl Legacy necklace, c. 2000s, cluster with glass beads, briolette crystals, and seed beads with classic baroque pearl and snake chain tassel below, toggle closure, marked Miriam Haskell, 34" long with 10 1/4" tassel. **$600-$700**

Author's Collection

Miriam Haskell Christmas tree pin, c. 2000s, red glass cabochons with clear rhinestone candles and rose montee star topper, made by Haskell designer Millie Petronzio, marked Miriam Haskell, 3 1/4" long.
$225-$275

Jewelry courtesy ChicAntiques.com

ABOVE Miriam Haskell bracelet, c. 1950s, leaf encrusted with clear rose montee rhinestones with baroque faux pearls, marked Miriam Haskell, bracelet 6 3/4" long with 1 3/4" leaf dangle.
$350-$400

Jewelry courtesy ChicAntiques.com

Miriam Haskell stickpin set, c. 1960s, green swirled glass elements with rhinestones and faux pearl accents, marked Miriam Haskell, pin 3 3/4" long, earrings 1 1/4" long.
$350-$500

Jewelry courtesy LinsyJsJewels.com

RIGHT Miriam Haskell brooch, c. 1950s, red glass roses amid brass findings with red rhinestones, marked Miriam Haskell, 4 1/4" wide. **$450-$550**

Jewelry courtesy LinsyJsJewels.com

ABOVE Miriam Haskell hinged cuff bracelet, c. 1960s, jewel-tone stained glass elements with matching seed beads, marked Miriam Haskell, 1 5/8" wide. **$325-$450**

Jewelry courtesy LinsyJsJewels.com

RIGHT Miriam Haskell necklace set, c. 1950s, pink swirled glass beads with floral centerpiece accented with rose montee rhinestones and opaque flat back stones, marked Miriam Haskell, necklace 19 1/2" long with 2 7/8" centerpiece, earrings 1 1/4". **$1,200-$1,500**

Jewelry courtesy LinsyJsJewels.com

HOBÉ

DESIGNERS AND MANUFACTURERS

Jewels of legendary splendor, the tagline used in Hobé advertising, certainly sums up the company's early work in America. Pieces made from the late 1920s through the 1930s by William Hobé's company were finely crafted in the Hobé family tradition using intricate settings, braided metalwork, and colorful unfoiled stones. These pieces have a Victorian revival air about them, and they're highly prized by collectors today. Some of the early Hobé designs are unmarked but many times can be identified by their construction.

Some pieces in similar styles to the early jewelry, with updated stones and colors, were advertised in 1948 as well. In fact, actress Ava Gardner was depicted wearing Hobé jewelry on the cover of *Photoplay* in December of that year.

From 1941 until after World War II, Hobé made sterling silver jewelry. This includes the popular Ming series of pins featuring Asian motifs. Bow pins and flower sprays are the most commonly found 1940s sterling items, and those with stones are more highly valued than plain pieces. Prices in general for these items have risen of late after a slump of several years.

Changing with the times, Hobé made many rhinestone jewelry pieces and beaded sets during the 1950s and 1960s. The company used a patented roller clip back on its earrings during this era. Many less interesting pendant necklaces and all-metal pieces were sold in the 1970s.

Collectors should also keep in mind that many pieces of low- to mid-grade costume jewelry were made in the early 2000s bearing the Hobé name but were not made by this company. They aren't technically reproductions, but rather fantasy or counterfeit pieces because they aren't duplicates of designs ever marketed by Hobé under its brand.

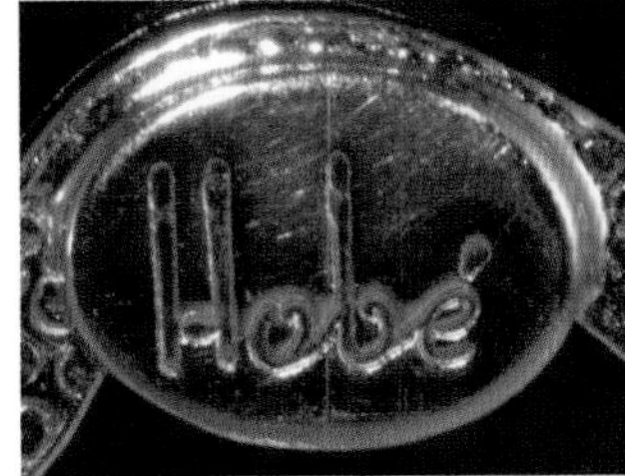

Hobé pastel necklace, c. late 1940s, pastel rhinestones in green, yellow, pink, and pale blue, 16" long with 1 7/8" drops. **$425-$550**

Jewelry courtesy LinsyJsJewels.com

ABOVE Hobé sterling spray brooch, c. 1940s, pink, yellow, blue, and red rhinestones set amid sterling silver leaves with bow embellishment, marked Hobé Sterling, 3 1/2" long. **$165-$195**

Jewelry courtesy ChicAntiques.com

RIGHT Hobé brooch, c. 1940s, sterling silver dove with pink and purple stones set in the wings holding dangling green rhinestone-embellished bow with tassels, marked Hobé Sterling, 3 1/4" long. **$175-$225**

Jewelry courtesy ChicAntiques.com

Hobé hematite chain necklace set, c. 1960s, gunmetal gray festoon-style chain necklace with matching earrings incorporating hematite and cranberry red rhinestones, marked Hobé, necklace 16" long, earrings 1 1/2" long.
$250-$350

Jewelry courtesy LinsyJsJewels.com

LEFT Hobé sterling flower bracelet, c. 1940s, brilliant blue rhinestones, marked Hobé Sterling, 7" long x 1" wide.
$155-$185

Jewelry courtesy ChicAntiques.com

BELOW Hobé sterling silver bracelet, c. 1940s, seven butterflies wide, marked Hobé Sterling, 7 1/4" long x 1" wide.
$135-$155

Jewelry courtesy ChicAntiques.com

Hobé glass rock necklace, c. late 1950s-early 1960s, pink and purple molded glass stones made to resemble quartz and amethyst with clear rhinestone accents and gold-tone settings, marked Hobé, adjusts from 14 1/2" to 17" long. **$235-$275**

Jewelry courtesy ChicAntiques.com

Hobé mesh necklace, c. late 1950s-early 1960s, silver-tone metal mesh wrapped with light and sapphire blue rhinestones, silver-tone beads with blue rhinestone embellishments dangle below, marked Hobé, 16" long. **$100-$125**

Jewelry courtesy ChicAntiques.com

Hobé cameo earrings, c. late 1950s-early 1960s, iridescent cameo centers surrounded by gray and yellow rhinestones, marked Hobé, 1 1/4" long. **$75-$95**

Jewelry courtesy ChicAntiques.com

Hobé brooch, c. 1960s, cat's eye foiled cabochons with royal blue rhinestones in pear and round shapes in heavily silver-plated setting indicative of 1960s manufacture, marked Hobé, 2 3/4" wide. **$100-$125**

Jewelry courtesy ChicAntiques.com

Hobé bandora brooch, c. 1947-1948, sterling silver with gold plating setting holds a standing Asian figure molded of resin to resemble Chinese bandora wood, marked Hobé 1/20th 14 kt. on Sterling, 2 1/4". **$250-$300**

Jewelry courtesy ChicAntiques.com

JOSEFF OF HOLLYWOOD

DESIGNERS AND MANUFACTURERS

Joseff of Hollywood is a familiar brand to most collectors, and the movie star jewelry in its archives is nothing short of extraordinary. Fortunate attendees of the Costume Jewelry Collectors International convention in 2011 got a taste of this grandeur as Michelle Joseff, granddaughter of Eugene and Joan Castle Joseff, and her mother, Tina Joseff, treated attendees to a display of pieces actually worn in films such as "Gone with the Wind," "Gentlemen Prefer Blonds," and "Cleopatra," along with many others.

Eugene Joseff was instrumental in costuming movies in Hollywood from 1928 until his untimely death in 1948 when his wife, Joan Castle, took the company reigns. She continued her husband's legacy of providing period-appropriate jewelry rentals to all the major Hollywood studios while also running the foundry, established during World War II, which produced airplane parts. The jewelry crafted by Joseff of Hollywood, both before Eugene's death and after, was made using matte Russian gold plating that played perfectly under Hollywood lighting.

The company also branched out in the late 1930s to create a retail line of jewelry that was sold in major department stores like Saks Fifth Avenue, I. Magnin, Bullock's, Neiman Marcus, Marshall Fields, and Nordstrom's. Eugene flew from city to city, delivering packages of Joseff jewelry to garner publicity for the new venture, and he was instrumental in helping to put together elaborate window displays showing off these glamorous styles. Joan continued to promote the retail jewelry business after she took over the company.

Joseff of Hollywood pieces, marked Joseff Hollywood in block letters, from the late 1930s and 1940s, are hard to find today. A *New York Times* article in 1950, based on an interview with Joan Castle Joseff, reported, "As with everything seen on the screen, Joseff creations, too, influence fashion. The more successful pieces are adapted for the 'commercial line' – sold in one big store in each city." These items were made in quantities in the thousands, according to Tina Joseff, which is quite low compared to larger manufacturers of costume jewelry doing business at that time. Add in the limited distribution, and it's understandable why these pieces don't crop up for collectors to find every day.

With very rare exception, the movie jewelry does not surface on the secondary collectibles market. If a piece is being sold as an original related to a specific star or movie, verifiable provenance should come along with it. Pieces in the retail line were generally not quite as elaborate as the movie pieces, although there were some exact copies made based on actual jewelry worn in films.

Joseff of Hollywood is still marketing jewelry today. These are not reproductions, but actual items being sold from the Joseff warehouse. Some complete pieces from the original retail lines with the old Joseff Hollywood mark are being discovered in the warehouse. Others are being made (and have been for quite some time) with original vintage components and stones purchased by Eugene Joseff and warehoused since the 1930s and 1940s. They are plated using the same technique and formula developed by Joseff more than 70 years ago.

All the newer pieces are marked with the round signature plaque except for items like the exotic jeweled elephant brooch in which the mark is incised into the metal. The most telltale sign of a more recent Joseff piece is the plating. Even though the secret Russian gold-plating formula is still used, the older pieces develop a patina over time that only comes with true aging. Some newer styles are variations of older pieces that are slightly modified; others are completely retired, as the company's stockpile of vintage components is depleted. Joseff also reported in 2013 that it is no longer using silver-plating on jewelry it produces.

While there has been some concern that the value of Joseff jewelry is being hurt by the recent influx of jewelry from the warehouse into the collectibles marketplace, this hasn't happened thus far. Joseff of Hollywood is largely a volume wholesaler, and when it sells directly, it rarely undercuts pricing, so values have remained strong for both vintage and newer pieces.

The advantage of Joseff using the components in its warehouse to create more jewelry actually fills a void and continues Eugene Joseff's retail philosophy, "... for movies, for stars, and for you." More people wanting to add a special Joseff piece to their collections can now have access to those items – they are usually considered a splurge since very few of them come inexpensively, regardless of the age.

In 2013 a new Joseff website was launched at www.joseffjewelry.com. The licensing agreement mentioned on the new site is geared toward manufacturers who might want to use old Joseff designs of either movie jewelry that was never part of the retail line, or retired pieces from the retail line, to create jewelry in larger quantities than the company is staffed to produce at this time. This may very well end up being fine jewelry rather than costume since the Joseffs will have final oversight of the production, and the quality will have to be high to get approval on any lines that may be authorized. The company will continue to market Joseff pieces from its warehouse stock, just as they always have.

LEFT Joseff earrings, c. 2000s, assembled by Joseff of Hollywood with vintage components, Russian gold-tone-plated metal set with emerald green and clear rhinestones, marked Joseff, 3 1/2" long. **$200-$250**

Jewelry courtesy ChicAntiques.com

ABOVE Joseff brooch, c. 1940s, silver-tone metal in impressive Victorian revival floral design, marked Joseff Hollywood, 3" wide. **$175-$225**

Jewelry courtesy ChicAntiques.com

ABOVE Joseff tassel brooch/pendant, c. 1940s, Russian gold-plated metal with bezel-set purple and clear unfoiled stones, marked Joseff Hollywood, pendant 6" long, can be removed from 22" neck chain and worn as a brooch. **$650-$750**

Author's Collection

RIGHT Joseff salamander necklace set, c. 2000s, assembled by Joseff of Hollywood with vintage components, Russian gold-tone-plated metal set with simulated turquoise scarabs, marked Joseff, adjusts to 19 1/2", each salamander dangle 2 7/8" long. **$650-$775**

Jewelry courtesy ChicAntiques.com

RIGHT Joseff butterfly necklace, c. 2000s, assembled by Joseff of Hollywood with vintage components, Russian gold-tone-plated metal set with royal blue and clear rhinestones, marked Joseff, 18 1/2" long with 3 1/2" butterfly. **$325-$400**

Jewelry courtesy ChicAntiques.com

ABOVE Joseff earrings, c. 2000s, assembled by Joseff of Hollywood with vintage components, Russian gold-tone-plated metal tops set with royal blue rhinestones with blue bezel set antique glass dangles, marked Joseff, 2 1/2" long. **$200-$250**

Jewelry courtesy ChicAntiques.com

LEFT Joseff bracelet, c. 1940s, Russian gold-plated metal with purple and clear unfoiled stones, marked Joseff Hollywood, 7 1/2" long x just under 1" wide. **$375-$450**

Author's Collection

ABOVE Joseff brooch, c. 1940s, Russian gold-tone-plated metal leaves surrounding large purple glass flower petals, marked Joseff Hollywood, just under 4" long. **$650-$750**

Author's Collection

LEFT Joseff cherub necklace, c. 2000s, assembled by Joseff of Hollywood with vintage components, Russian gold-tone-plated metal set with ruby red glass bullet cabochons and faux pearls, marked Joseff, adjusts to 19 1/2". **$500-$625**

Jewelry courtesy ChicAntiques.com

BELOW Joseff elephant brooch, c. 1950s, Russian gold-tone-plated metal set with jewel-tone rhinestones and faux pearl accents, marked Joseff, 2" long. **$275-$325**

Jewelry courtesy ChicAntiques.com

GEMSCOPE
an in-depth look

How Old is Your Joseff of Hollywood jewelry?

Joseff of Hollywood jewelry sold through its retail lines is divided in age between the earliest "Joseff Hollywood" pieces and the later round "Joseff" mark. Since Joseff is still using the same secret Russian matte finish gold-plating formula on jewelry made with old stones and components warehoused by Eugene Joseff in the late 1930s and early 1940s, it's often the patina that only age can impart to a finish that sets the round marked pieces apart.

Jewelry courtesy ChicAntiques.com

MARK TOP **Old mark dating to the late 1930s, early 1940s.**

MARK RIGHT **Mark found on 1950s cross pendant shown below.**

MARK FAR RIGHT **Mark found on 2000s cherub brooch shown below.**

Fleur de lis dress clip from around 1940 bearing the old "Joseff Hollywood" mark. $125-175

Rhinestone cross pendant marked "Joseff" likely dating to the 1950s; cross 3" long. $275-350

Cherub brooch is also marked "Joseff," a newer production piece made with old components; 2 3/8" wide. $150-185

Joseff necklace, c. 2000s, Russian gold-tone calla lily stampings with purple and clear rhinestones in a grand Victorian revival design, marked Joseff, 17" long x 3 5/8" wide. **$875-$1,000**

Jewelry courtesy ChicAntiques.com

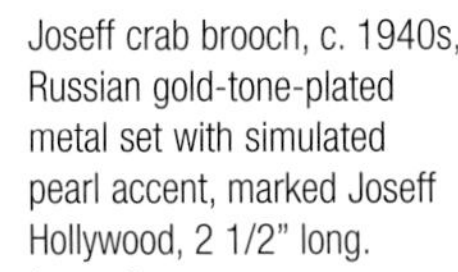

Joseff crab brooch, c. 1940s, Russian gold-tone-plated metal set with simulated pearl accent, marked Joseff Hollywood, 2 1/2" long. **$225-$275**

Jewelry courtesy ChicAntiques.com

Joseff sun god brooch, c. 1940s, copy of Joan Castle's favorite brooch fashioned for her of 18 karat gold and diamonds by her husband Eugene Joseff. This one features Russian gold-tone-plated metal and dangling rhinestone eyes, marked Joseff Hollywood, just under 4" long. **$275-$300**

Author's Collection

KENNETH JAY LANE

DESIGNERS AND MANUFACTURERS

Kenneth Jay Lane's jewelry-related career dates back to 1962 when he launched his first lines. He sees his jewelry as "art that becomes reality when worn by people." He found inspiration through other designers such as Fulco Di Verdura, and other designers following him have in turn been inspired by his work. His designs also include influences gleaned from Asia, India, and the crown jewels.

The large and showy earrings and necklaces he designed in the 1960s are favorites of collectors today, and they can be quite costly to obtain. His jewelry was popular back when it was new, too, with everyone from royalty, both the British and Hollywood varieties, to First Ladies being photographed wearing K.J.L.

Most folks who aren't avid collectors, however, know him through his association with the television shopping channel QVC since the early 1990s, and prior to that his popular lines sold through Avon beginning in the mid-1980s. The earlier Avon jewelry is of surprisingly good quality, and some of the pieces are indeed considered collectible today. Newer lines being marketed under his brand are available at varying price points, and some are more nicely crafted than others. The upscale lines offered through retailers like Neiman Marcus are generally nice, and many of them have collectible attributes.

For an overview of Kenneth Jay Lane's career in the jewelry business through the mid-1990s, look for a copy of the currently out-of-print book *Faking It* by Kenneth Jay Lane and Harrice Simmons Miller. In addition to some interesting anecdotes from Lane, the photos included tell the story quite well.

The earliest Kenneth Jay Lane jewelry is usually marked "K.J.L." with periods separating the initials (Figure 1). These shouldn't be confused with later jewelry marked "©KJL" without periods between the letters (Figure 2), used on QVC pieces as well as other newer pieces sold in boutiques and upscale department stores. The craftsmanship and style of the earlier pieces has a less mass-produced look, but most of these pieces are still high in quality. Another mark used during the early years spelled out Kenneth Lane curving around a copyright symbol

FIGURE 1

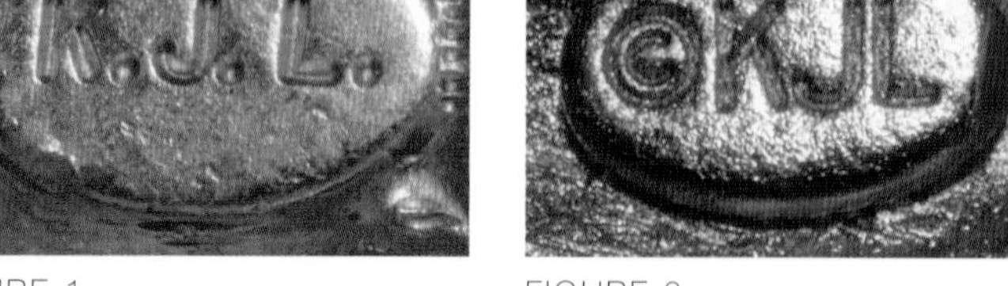

FIGURE 2

FIGURE 3

within an oval cartouche (not shown). A similar mark is used today, with "Kenneth" curved at the top of the oval and "©Lane" curved at the bottom (Figure 3).

Many pieces of low- to mid-end costume jewelry were made in the early 2000s bearing the Kenneth Jay Lane (whether as K.J.L. or Kenneth Lane) name that were not made by this company. They aren't technically reproductions, but rather fantasy or counterfeit pieces because they aren't duplicates of designs ever marketed by Kenneth Lane under his brand.

Kenneth Jay Lane necklace, c. mid-2000s, five strands of faux pearls with large rhinestone rose clasp, marked ©KJL, 18" long with 2" clasp.
$325-$375

Jewelry courtesy ChicAntiques.com

ABOVE Kenneth Jay Lane salamander brooch, c. 2000s, green enameled gold-tone metal with red and clear rhinestones, marked Kenneth ©Lane, 3 3/4" long. **$250-$350**

Jewelry courtesy LinsyJsJewels.com

Kenneth Jay Lane necklace set, c. 2000s, clear navette rhinestones set in polished gold-tone metal, marked Kenneth ©Lane. **$525-$700**

Jewelry courtesy LinsyJsJewels.com

Kenneth Jay Lane snake bracelet, c. 2000s, faux turquoise beads with red square-cut rhinestones and clear accents, marked Kenneth ©Lane, contemporary coiled hinge. **$450-$575**

Jewelry courtesy LinsyJsJewels.com

LEFT Kenneth Jay Lane frog brooch, c. late 1960s, gold-tone body encrusted with clear rhinestones, faux jade back, red rhinestone eyes, marked K.J.L, 1 5/8" long. **$100-$135**

Jewelry courtesy LinsyJsJewels.com

Kenneth Jay Lane Jackie O star brooch, c. early 1990s, matte gold-tone star with multicolor rhinestones, brooch originally designed for Jackie Onassis, purchased at The Smithsonian in the early 1990s, marked Kenneth ©Lane, 3 5/8" long. **$175-$225**

Author's Collection

FAR LEFT Kenneth Jay Lane kissing monkey bracelets, c. mid-2000s, hinged cuff bracelets with contemporary coil hinge, gold-tone heads with clear collars and emerald green rhinestone eyes, one with brown enamel and one with black and white harlequin-patterned enamel, marked ©KJL, 1/2" wide. **$75-$125 each**

Author's Collection

Kenneth Jay Lane Art Deco revival brooch, c. 1990s, acrylic resin fashioned to simulate onyx and coral with molded jade glass and square rhinestone accents on silver-tone setting, marked Kenneth ©Lane, 2 1/2" long. **$125-$150**

Jewelry courtesy ChicAntiques.com

KRAMER OF NEW YORK

DESIGNERS AND MANUFACTURERS

The Diamond Look" by Kramer slogan has been noted on original packaging, tags marking jewelry, and in advertising campaigns of the 1940s and 1950s. Some of the early jewelry made by this company, founded by Louis Kramer in 1943 and in business through 1980, did indeed have a fine jewelry look about it. What collectors find most often today, however, are frankly fake rhinestone designs from the 1950s and 1960s.

Jewelry is marked Kramer or Kramer of New York in a variety of ways. How a piece is marked doesn't affect its value as much as the overall style, quality, and type of components used. Pieces incorporating molded glass leaves, specialty stones, and colorful dangling balls or crystals are some of the most desirable pieces, along with larger necklace styles.

Attributing one particular style to this company is all but impossible, and pegging unmarked pieces as Kramer is very difficult unless you've actually seen matching pieces marked as such. Some of the stones used in Kramer pieces overlap with other brands, as do the way the pieces were constructed, making them rather generic. Much of the nicest Kramer jewelry does sell for good sums, especially the Christian Dior by Kramer lines dating to the 1950s, but there are still some beautiful pieces that are quite undervalued, waiting to be added to collections.

Amourelle, a 1960s line designed by Frank Hess for Kramer after he left Miriam Haskell, also has a following among collectors. Most of those pieces readily show their Hess touch, and many favor Haskell designs over Kramer's traditional "Diamond Look" glitz.

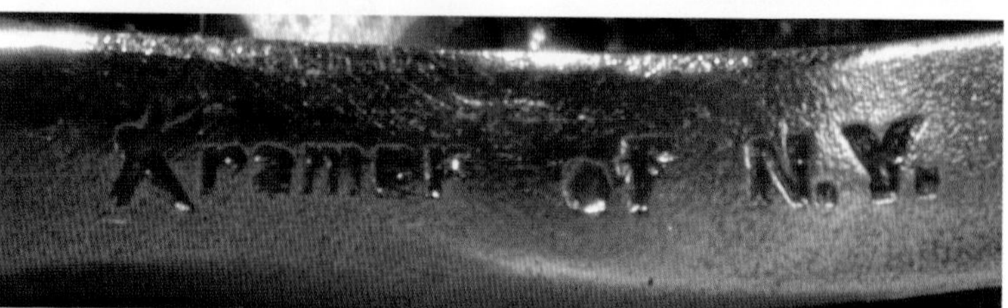

Kramer Victorian revival necklace, c. late 1950s, aurora borealis rhinestones in pear and round shapes with clear accents in Victorian revival style antiqued gold-tone setting, marked Kramer of New York, necklace 15 3/4" long with 2" centerpiece. **$175-$225**

Author's Collection

Kramer bracelet, c. 1960s, gray and aurora borealis emerald-cut rhinestones with gold-plated setting, each row of stones moves independently, marked Kramer, 7" long x 1" wide. **$125-$175**

Author's Collection

Kramer bracelet set, c. 1950s, large glass stones 1" long with clear accents in silver-tone setting, marked Kramer of New York, bracelet 7 1/2" long x 7/8" wide, earrings 1" long. **$65-$95**

Author's Collection

Kramer necklace, c. late 1950s, light brown and topaz rhinestones with aurora borealis accents in semi-collar style, marked Kramer, 16 1/4" long x 1 3/4" wide. **$165-$195**

Author's Collection

Kramer sapphire rhinestone bracelet, c. early 1950s, blue navette flowers with brilliant clear accents in rhodium-plated setting, 6 7/8" long. **$100-$125**

Jewelry courtesy ChicAntiques.com

BELOW Kramer bracelet, c. 1950s, sapphire blue cabochons and bright blue rhinestones surround vivid foiled and iridescent cabochons in antiqued silver-tone setting, 7 1/4" long. **$150-$175**

Jewelry courtesy ChicAntiques.com

ABOVE Kramer bracelet, c. 1950s, clear frosted glass blue and clear bicolor leaves with dangling iridescent crystal and light blue beads, rhinestones are gray navettes and clear chatons in antiqued silver-tone setting, marked Kramer of N.Y, 7 1/4" long x 1 3/8" wide. **$185-$225**

Author's Collection

RIGHT Kramer set, c. late 1950s, elongated iridescent glass leaves with blue rhinestones in varying shades and aurora borealis accents, finely cast and finished domed silver-tone setting on brooch, marked Kramer, brooch 2 3/8" wide, earrings 1 1/4". **$135-$165**

Author's Collection

Kramer brooch set, c. 1950s, clear frosted glass leaves with dangling iridescent crystal beads and clear rhinestones set in antiqued silver-tone metal, articulated so that the bottom sections dangle, marked Kramer, brooch 3 1/4" long. **$200-$250**

Author's Collection

ABOVE Kramer bracelet, c. 1950s, blue button pearls surrounded by blue, green, and red rhinestones, marked Kramer of New York, 7" long x 1" wide. **$250-$325**

Jewelry courtesy LinsyJsJewels.com

RIGHT Kramer bracelet, c. late 1950s, elongated iridescent molded glass leaves and frosted bicolor leaves with red, pink, and purple rhinestones in varied shapes and sizes, finely cast and finished gold-tone setting, marked Kramer of N.Y, 7 1/4" long x 1 1/8" wide. **$195-$225**

Kramer brooch, c. late 1950s, elongated iridescent molded glass leaves with red and purple rhinestones in varied shapes and sizes, finely cast and finished domed gold-tone setting, marked Kramer, 2 3/8" wide. **$125-$145**

Author's Collection

RIGHT Kramer earrings, c. 1958, clear rhinestones with emerald green glass bead dangles, 2 1/2" long. **$175-$200**

Jewelry courtesy ChicAntiques.com

FAR RIGHT Kramer brooch, c. late 1950s, elongated iridescent molded glass leaves with brown, green, and orange rhinestones in varying shapes and sizes, finely cast and finished gold-tone setting, marked Kramer, brooch 3 1/4" long. **$100-$135**

Author's Collection

MAZER/JOMAZ

DESIGNERS AND MANUFACTURERS

Joseph and Louis Mazer founded the company bearing their family name in the late 1920s. Together they manufactured finely crafted jewelry under the Mazer brand. Many early Mazer pieces were unmarked, but if a patent number is present on the mechanisms or components, they often can be identified and dated with a bit of online research. Marcel Boucher worked as a designer for the company prior to founding his own costume jewelry business in 1937, and his name can be found on some of the design patents issued to Mazer.

During the mid-1940s the brothers split up. What came after is often confusing to collectors. There are many iterations of information both online and in print pertaining to Joseph and Louis Mazer's respective businesses, and much of it is only partially true.

Louis Mazer worked with his son, Nat, to continue the company he founded in the 1920s with his brother. Jewelry made while they were still together was marked MAZER (in block letters). Jewelry made from 1946-1951 was marked MAZER BROS., even though the brothers were no longer working together. All patents for Mazer jewelry belong to Mazer Bros., and none were issued after 1950, according to research and examples gathered by jewelry historian Robin Deutsch.

Joseph Mazer founded a new company after leaving Mazer Bros., and by the late 1940s he was designing jewelry collections under his new brand: Jomaz. In fact, *Women's Wear Daily* introduced his showroom and jewelry in an article dated 1949. The business produced jewelry through the early 1980s. The Jomaz mark was used on most pieces, but a few have been found signed Joseph Mazer. Items marked Adolfo for Mazer are later pieces made in the years just prior to the company's closing.

Much of the early jewelry made by Mazer, signed or unsigned, is very highly regarded among collectors and quite hard to find today. What complicates matters is that many copies of early Mazer designs have been produced over the decades since the 1930s. This includes both pot metal

Mazer earrings, c. early 1940s, molded blue glass leaf-shaped stones and blue glass moonstone cabochons with clear rhinestone accents in rhodium-plated settings, marked Mazer, 1" long.
$95-$125

Jewelry courtesy ChicAntiques.com

copies made during the same period, like the lesser-quality pieces Reinad marketed then, and later reproductions with more modern construction and plating.

Mazer's famous mask designs readily come to mind here. If you have an unsigned mask in a style similar to a Mazer patent, and it has a pin back and gold-tone plating, this is a newer piece of costume jewelry. An original Mazer Bros. mask would have a pin clip (also known as a fur clip) mechanism and be finely rhodium-plated. The newer pieces certainly can be attractive to wear, but they shouldn't be sold as original Mazer pieces.

RIGHT Mazer Retro parure, c. late 1930s-early 1940s, emerald green glass stones with clear rhinestone accents, marked Mazer, 3" wide. **$325-$400**

Jewelry courtesy LinsyJsJewels.com

BELOW Jomaz bracelet set, c. 1960s, simulated glass jade and turquoise cabochons with clear rhinestone accents, marked Jomaz, bracelet 7 1/4" long, earrings 1". **$500-$650**

Jewelry courtesy LinsyJsJewels.com

Mazer brooch, c. 1940s, red, clear, and blue rhinestones set in sterling silver Retro Moderne setting, marked Mazer and Sterling, 3" wide. **$325-$400**

Jewelry courtesy LinsyJsJewels.com

Jomaz brooch, c. 1950s, simulated aquamarine blue unfoiled stones with pavé-set clear rhinestone accents set in gold-plated metal, marked Jomaz, 2" wide. **$125-$175**

Jewelry courtesy ChicAntiques.com

LEFT Jomaz flower vase set, c. late 1950s, blue glass moonstone cabochons with red, blue, and clear rhinestone embellishments in rhodium-plated settings, marked Jomaz, 2" long, earrings 1". **$175-$200**

Jewelry courtesy ChicAntiques.com

BELOW Jomaz bracelet, c. 1950s, sapphire blue glass stones with rhinestone accents in rhodium-plated setting, marked Jomaz, 7 1/4" long. **$375-$450**

Jewelry courtesy LinsyJsJewels.com

GEMSCOPE
an in-depth look

Mazer Double Clip Enamel Bracelet c.1936

This unsigned Art Deco hinged cuff bracelet by Mazer features enamel over rhodium-plated metal. The bracelet has two detachable rhinestone clips that may be removed and worn separately. This piece was designed by Marcel Boucher for Mazer prior to his departure to begin his own jewelry firm in 1937. The clips are rhodium-plated base metal set with bead and bezel set round, baguette, and hexagonal-shaped clear rhinestones. Based on Utility Patent 2034129 for a double clip brooch filed on Nov. 1, 1935 and awarded to Marcel Boucher on March 17, 1936, this bracelet was inspired by similar Cartier bracelets made during the same timeframe, according to jewelry historian Robin Deutsch. These pieces are exceptionally rare as they are always unsigned and usually misattributed. Most likely when they were sold, the separate mechanism to join them together to make a brooch was included with the bracelet (similar to Trifari Clip-Mate bracelets also sold during the 1930s). When the clips are attached to the mechanism, they face the opposite way from the bracelet, so it makes a slightly different design than when attached to a "double clip brooch" (referenced by collectors by the generic name "duette"). Any Mazer double clip brooch can be used on bracelets with this patent number, as the clip back mechanisms are exactly the same. There are a few Mazer double clip brooch utility patents, designed by Boucher with the assignor as Mazer, that are virtually the same and utilize a similar dress clip finding, and each patent shows a slight improvement upon the prior. The number will be found stamped on the clip mechanism. Made for a small wrist, but depending on which clips are used, the bracelet has some flexibility in size. Bangle is 1" wide; each dress clip is 1 1/4" x 1 1/4". **$1,250-$1,500**

Jewelry courtesy Robin Deutsch Collection

Jomaz earrings, c. late 1950s, open-backed simulated flawed emeralds framed by clear rhinestones in rhodium-plated settings, marked Jomaz, 3/4" long. **$75-$95**

Jewelry courtesy ChicAntiques.com

LEFT Jomaz snake necklace, c. 1960s, green and blue enamel and clear rhinestone accents on gold-tone metal with simulated pearls, marked Jomaz, 16"long. **$225-$275**

Jewelry courtesy ChicAntiques.com

Jomaz earrings, c. late 1950s, open-backed jewel-tone rhinestones of emerald green, ruby red, sapphire blue, amethyst purple, and topaz yellow set in rhodium-plated metal, marked Jomaz, 7/8"long. **$75-$95**

Jewelry courtesy ChicAntiques.com

Jomaz necklace, c. 1950s, cranberry red, green, purple, and blue open-backed molded glass stones with clear rhinestone and faux pearl accents in rhodium-plated metal, marked Jomaz, 15 1/2" long. **$150-$200**

Jewelry courtesy ChicAntiques.com

NAPIER

DESIGNERS AND MANUFACTURERS

One of the most common misconceptions about Napier jewelry revolves around boredom. Because the Napier jewelry commonly found today is rather boring stuff made during the company's later years, folks tend to lump it all into that category. The truth is that Napier made some interesting, gorgeous, and finely crafted jewelry throughout its lengthy run in the jewelry business.

Since this company was around for so long, starting out as E.A. Bliss in 1878, this section serves to hit the high points and share some introductory information designed to whet your appetite for more Napier learning. For instance, early Napier earrings were made only in amber but could be special ordered in other colors. Finding early pieces with Victorian and Edwardian influences dating to the 1920s-1930s isn't any easy feat, however, and the marks Napier used back then are very similar to those used in the 1950s, and even in later years in a few instances. You absolutely have to look at the styles, components, and construction when dating Napier pieces.

Another fact that collectors sometimes skate over with Napier is that it produced some incredible "boutique" lines in the 1950s and 1960s. These pieces incorporate finely crafted, heavily plated metalwork with brilliant stones, albeit sometimes sparsely set in comparison to other lines from this era. Nevertheless, the jewelry is outstanding in terms of quality and construction, and it wore well over time. These pieces are easily confused with newer Napier because they held up so nicely and the designs were quite often ahead of their time.

Some of Napier's most popular designs in the 1950s were charm bracelets. The "Tropicana" model dating to 1955 featured "Moonglow" pearlized Lucite beads in stylized fruit shapes with earrings to match. Asian motifs were also popular for charm-style bracelets. Others were made of miscellaneous charms left over from other designs, and these can be truly unique finds. Early 1970s charm bracelets with the Napier brand tend to feature one dangling element such as the popular "Wedding Bell" with a crystal clapper or a bejeweled elephant.

Beware of Napier being marketed as sterling silver, including charm bracelets, if the item is not plainly marked. This is one company that almost never used sterling for jewelry manufacture without marking it as such. They did use very heavy silver plating, and this sometimes tests as sterling with the

Napier bracelet, c. 1960s, gold-tone rope chains and brown moonglow beads with grape cluster comprised of gold-tone beads, moonglow beads, and large stamped leaves, marked Napier. **$175-$225**

Jewelry courtesy ChicAntiques.com

traditional scratch and acid drop testing most people use, including fine jewelers who might be asked to evaluate Napier from time to time. Fine jewelers of today aren't really up on the manufacturing techniques used to make this type of jewelry, so mistakes can be made.

In fact, if you find a piece of genuine Napier that isn't marked at all, this is by and large an anomaly. More often than not, unmarked jewelry that is purportedly Napier is being misidentified. Or the clasp where the Napier mark was originally found has been replaced. One way or another, a piece of jewelry represented as unsigned Napier should raise a red flag that something probably isn't quite right.

Napier made some really finely crafted lines from the 1970s on through the 1990s, and some of the best were limited editions. Not all 1970-1990s Napier is considered high-end collector caliber, but certain lines can be too nice to pass up when looking at the cast construction, heavy gold plating, and stone quality. This is a heads-up, by the way, for dealers who have traditionally shunned all of Napier's newer pieces.

You'll also notice that pieces with original foil hangtags still attached read "By Napier" on the front and "Est. 1875" on the back. In spite of this "confirmation" of Napier's start date, when doing research for "The Napier Co." author Melinda Lewis discovered by examining company records that the anniversary date was listed as 1878 through 1929. Then one document was found with 1878 crossed out and 1875 clearly penciled in. From the 1930s on, Napier's start date was consistently advertised as 1875.

Lewis's book, *The Napier Co.*, elaborates on the history of the company and the full spectrum of the lines it marketed, so for a full dose of Napier education be sure to order a copy online at www.napierbook.com. It's well worth the price and includes jewelry history worthy of note even beyond this copious brand.

Napier necklace, c. late-1920s, silver-tone filigree metal elements with blue glass beads, no clasp, fits over head to wear, marked Napier, 37 1/2" long with 3 1/2" pendant. **$200-$250**

Author's Collection

Napier interchangeable set, c. 1960s, gold-tone flower mountings with interchangeable screw-in clear rhinestones, pearls, and glass balls in dark green, turquoise blue, and coral in original fitted box, marked Napier ©, ring is adjustable in size, earrings 3/4" wide. **$125-$150**

Author's Collection

Napier collar necklace, c. 1995, part of the Black Tie collection, gold-tone setting with black and clear rhinestones, also made in multicolor variation in 1991, marketed as "Royalton," marked Napier in script.
$250-$300

Jewelry courtesy ChicAntiques.com

Napier Asian motif necklace, c. 1960s, gold-tone Asian medallions suspended from mother of pearl and simulated jade beads, marked Napier ©.
$125-$150

Jewelry courtesy ChicAntiques.com

Napier charm bracelet, c. 1950s, silver-plated with five charms: gryphon with armor, shell, fly, owl, and scarab, marked Napier, 7 3/4" long.
$150-$175

Author's Collection

ABOVE Napier earrings, c. 1950s, silver-plated clip earrings with dangling glass bead embellishments to match ram bracelet with original Napier tag, marked Napier Pat. Pend., 2 1/2" long. **$100-$125**

Author's Collection

RIGHT Napier ram bracelet, c. 1950s, silver-plated cuff bracelet with dangling glass bead and charm embellishments, marked Napier, 3 1/2" wide including dangling elements. **$475-$600**

Author's Collection

Napier basket earrings, c. 1950s, silver-plated flower and vine stampings with purple rhinestones in silver-tone settings beautifully finished on the front as well as the back, marked Napier, 1 1/8" wide. **$225-$275**

Author's Collection

Napier bracelet, c. late-1920s, gold-plated fine filigree metal with topaz glass bezel-set stones, fastens with hidden clasp, marked Napier, 7 1/4" long x 1 1/4" wide. **$200-$250**

Author's Collection

ABOVE Napier sterling Modernist necklace, c. early 1950s, stylized scallops with dangle drops suspended from serpentine chain, marked Napier Sterling, 16" long with 1 5/8" drops. **$135-$165**

Author's Collection

RIGHT Napier winged brooch set, c. 1950s, considered rare, matte with polished highlights gold-plated wing stampings with rhinestone chain embellishment and dangling pear-shaped stones, marked Napier, brooch 4" wide, earrings 3 5/8" long. **$225-$300**

Author's Collection

Napier set, c. 1990, part of the Napier Hollywood collection introduced in 1990, brilliant clear navette rhinestones in textured gold-tone metal, marked Napier in script, necklace 16 1/2" long, bracelet 7" long. **$125-$150**

Jewelry courtesy ChicAntiques.com

Napier parure, c. mid-1990s, matte gold-tone paisley shapes set with brilliant red and gray rhinestones, marked Napier in script. **$150-$200**

Jewelry courtesy ChicAntiques.com

Napier bracelet, c. early 1930s, gold-plated filigree hinged cuff bracelet with six unfoiled bezel-set square stones simulating aquamarine, marked Napier, 1 1/8" wide. **$225-$275**

Author's Collection

SCHIAPARELLI

DESIGNERS AND MANUFACTURERS

Italian-born designer Elsa Schiaparelli's early work was most definitely influenced by her years spent in Paris, with a nod toward the Surrealism and Dadaism movements she embraced there. In the late 1920s she hired Jean Clément to design jewelry for her couture house. She also worked with Roger Jean-Pierre in the 1940s and with Coppola e Toppo in the late 1940s and early 1950s. Many note Jean Schlumberger as her most creative designer, however. This is perhaps the high card played in Schiaparelli's rivalry with Coco Chanel, who employed Duke Falco di Verdura as her featured designer at that time.

Some of the most highly regarded pieces produced under Schiaparelli's direction, and most certainly prized by the lucky collectors who own them, were designed by Schlumberger. The "Circus Collection" and the "Pagan Collection" featured fanciful horses and other Big Top themes along with fruits, vegetables, and curling vines. Other figural brooches, buttons, and even cufflinks were made of enameled or plated metal and rhinestones in whimsical shapes featuring ocean themes and bird motifs. A pair of rare, fanciful enameled ostrich pendants with glass beads dangling around their necklines resides in the renowned Barbara Berger collection featured in a 2013 museum exhibit hosted by the Museum of Arts and Design in New York City, along with the related book. These rare pieces are not the type of Schiaparelli jewelry found by collectors today.

What we see offered for sale in all but rare instances are the pieces made in the United States from 1949 on. These are often bold designs with large stones that gained favor with the fashionable set moving into the 1950s. Some of these designs are more inspiring than others, and the price they command reflects their desirability among collectors. For example, common cluster bead earrings may sell for less than $50 while a pair incorporating iridescent "lava rock" or colorful kite-shaped stones can top $300, depending on the style.

Early jewelry produced by Elsa Schiaparelli's fashion house was marked Schiaparelli in lowercase block letters, and these pieces surface for sale occasionally. They were imported into the United States by the David Lisner Co. when they were new. Schiaparelli licensed Lisner to manufacture jewelry bearing her name in 1949 after fleeing Paris for New York due to German occupation earlier in the decade.

This jewelry, which is upscale in comparison to what collectors usually expect from Lisner, was marked with a script Schiaparelli signature or with a torso-shaped paper tag that resembled the packaging of the popular Shocking perfume. The backs of these Shocking pink tags read,

Schiaparelli brooch set, c. late 1950s-early 1960s, iridescent molded glass ovals with blue, green, and aurora borealis rhinestones in gold-plated setting, marked Schiaparelli, brooch 2 1/2" wide, earrings 1 1/8". **$200-$250**

Jewelry courtesy LinsyJsJewels.com

Schiaparelli necklace set, c. 1960s, necklace features "Shocking" pink and purple glass beads with rhinestone cluster worn to the side, matching earrings are comprised of bright pink, purple, and pink/light teal green bicolor rhinestones, marked Schiaparelli, necklace 16 1/2" long, earrings 1 1/2" long. **$575-700**

Jewelry courtesy LinsyJsJewels.com

"Designed in Paris ... Created in America ...." The tags were discarded when the jewelry was worn, so a designer piece then became unsigned. (For more information on identifying unsigned Schiaparelli jewelry with examples, see Section Three.)

It should also be noted jewelry marked "Schaperelli" (misspelled in block lettering) has also been found. While sometimes lovely, they are not authentic pieces made under the direction of the House of Schiaparelli and have been deemed reproductions meant to deceive collectors.

RIGHT Schiaparelli kite stones brooch, c. 1950s, sapphire, light blue, and gray unfoiled rhinestones with aurora borealis accents, marked Schiaparelli, 3" wide. **$325-$375**

Jewelry courtesy ChicAntiques.com

FAR RIGHT Schiaparelli angelfish brooch, c. late-1950s, simulated pearls and aurora borealis rhinestones in gunmetal setting, marked Schiaparelli, 2 3/4" long. **$200-$250**

Jewelry courtesy LinsyJsJewels.com

ABOVE Schiaparelli bracelet set, c. 1960s, orange molded glass beads with simulated pearls and ornate clasp featuring "lava rock" stones with aurora borealis accents, marked Schiaparelli, bracelet 7 1/4" long, earrings 2 3/4". **$650-$800**

Jewelry courtesy LinsyJsJewels.com

RIGHT Schiaparelli set, c. 1950s, pink molded glass stones surrounded by orange, pink, and purple rhinestones, marked Schiaparelli, brooch 3" wide, earrings 1 1/2" long. **$350-$400**

Jewelry courtesy ChicAntiques.com

Schiaparelli necklace, c. 1950s, bi-tone blue and clear swirled beads with large glass center stone surrounded by light blue rhinestones, marked Schiaparelli, 15 1/2" long with 2 1/4" centerpiece. **$250-$300**

Jewelry courtesy ChicAntiques.com

Schiaparelli earrings, c. 1960s, orange "lava rock" stones, molded glass, and white iridescent navettes, and round accents in orange and yellow, marked Schiaparelli, 1 1/2" long. **$175-$225**

Jewelry courtesy ChicAntiques.com

Schiaparelli bracelet set, c. 1950s, iridescent molded glass tulip-shaped stones with emerald green and sapphire blue rhinestones in gunmetal setting, marked Schiaparelli, bracelet 7" long, earrings 1 1/2". **$550-700**

Jewelry courtesy LinsyJsJewels.com

SCHREINER OF NEW YORK

DESIGNERS AND MANUFACTURERS

As the story goes, Henry Schreiner went from early 1900s blacksmith to shoe buckle fabricator to costume jeweler serving couture designers in both the United States and abroad. Jewelry marked Schreiner or Schreiner of New York, rarely advertised but shown on the cover of Vogue in December 1950, is known for incorporating amazing stone and color combinations into intricate and impressive designs. Many of the stones were made expressly for Schreiner, including the fabulous keystone-shaped rhinestones manufactured for use in its popular "ruffle" brooches.

After Henry Schreiner's death in 1954, his daughter and son-in-law continued to run the business through the mid- to late-1970s (some sources indicate 1975, others 1977). Pieces made in the 1960s and 1970s have a decidedly different look about them, with flower pins and earrings and pendant necklaces being prime examples, but all the jewelry made by this company was of very high quality.

Setting rhinestones, often unfoiled, with the pointed end up was a Schreiner construction staple. Newcomers to costume jewelry collecting sometimes confuse this construction with rivoli stones (see Section Three for an example). This company was reportedly one of the first to use dark gunmetal finishes, which allows richly colored stones to stand out among the settings. A number of highly collectible pieces combine faceted acrylic resin with unfoiled stones for looks that are uniquely Schreiner.

And while there has been no definite confirmation regarding some Schreiner of New York pieces being manufactured in Austria, especially those dating to the 1950s, pieces bearing very similar characteristics have been noted. Many Schreiner pieces have overlapping construction techniques and components with those marked "Made in Austria," including the familiar "donut hole" clip backs used on numerous earrings made by this company. (See examples of this clip back style in Section Three.)

The larger necklaces made by Schreiner are highly prized, and collectors will pay dearly to own them. Bracelets by this company are not plentiful and usually sell for good sums. Many Schreiner brooches are available, usually reasonably priced, depending on the demand at the moment. An impressive collection can be garnered by scouring the market for unsigned pieces as well (see Section Three for more information on identifying unsigned Schreiner, with numerous examples).

Schreiner brooch, c. 1950s, faux pearls and brilliant clear rhinestones, marked Schreiner New York, 3 7/8" long. **$225-$275**

Author's Collection

ABOVE Schreiner bracelet, c. late 1950s, blue cabochons with brilliant blue, green, and aurora borealis rhinestones in a silver-tone setting, marked Schreiner, 7 1/2" long x 7/8" wide. **$275-$325**

Author's Collection

LEFT Schreiner brooch, c. 1950s, round baroque pearl 1" wide surrounded by clear inverted rhinestones, back view shows how the large inverted stones wrap around the sides of the brooch, unmarked. **$225-$275**

Jewelry courtesy ChicAntiques.com

LEFT Schreiner Lucite brooch, c. 1960s, brown and clear acrylic resin teardrops with clear and brown inverted rhinestones in gold-plated setting, unmarked, 4 1/4" wide. **$275-$350**

Author's Collection

FAR LEFT Schreiner brooch, c. 1950s, emerald green art glass drops, faux pearls, and clear inverted rhinestones, may also be worn as a pendant, marked Schreiner New York, 3 7/8" long. **$275-$325**

Author's Collection

Schreiner insect pin, c. 1950s, oval simulated turquoise art glass cabochon inverted fuchsia and gray rhinestones, unmarked. **$125-$145**

Jewelry courtesy ChicAntiques.com

ABOVE Schreiner necklace/brooch, c. 1950s, amber art glass drops, faux pearls, and topaz glass beads with gray inverted unfoiled rhinestones, pendant may be removed from chain and worn as a brooch, unmarked, neck chain adjusts to 19 1/2" long, pendant/brooch 5 1/2" long x 3 1/2" wide. **$750-$900**

Author's Collection

RIGHT Schreiner Lucite Maltese cross brooch, c. 1960s, clear acrylic resin teardrops and clear inverted rhinestones in gold-plated setting with leaf findings, unmarked, 3 3/8" wide. **$250-$300**

Author's Collection

Schreiner spray brooch, c. 1950s, clear and champagne rhinestones with simulated pearls in gold-tone setting, marked Schreiner New York, 3 1/2" wide. **$275-$350**

Author's Collection

ABOVE Schreiner collar necklace, c. 1950s, painted and foiled cabochons with a variety of rhinestones, shapes, and sizes in blue and green colorations along with simulated pearl accents, marked Schreiner, 15 1/2" long x 2" wide. **$1,100-$1,200**

Author's Collection

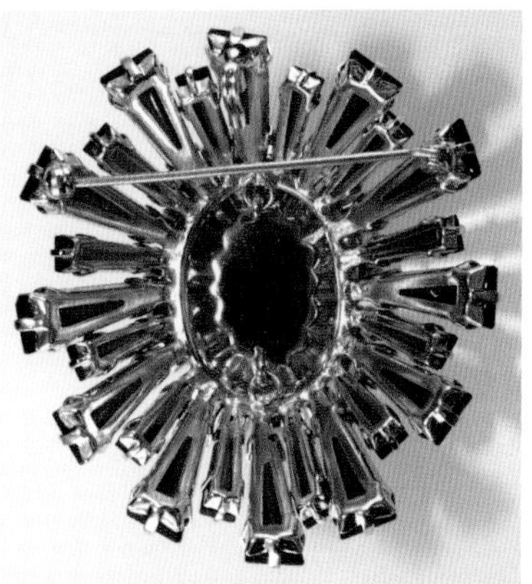

LEFT Schreiner brooch, c. 1950s, purple keystone rhinestones in a variation of the popular "ruffle" brooch, center is an oval purple art glass stone surrounded by inverted simulated turquoise stones, unmarked, 2 1/4" long x 1 1/4" deep. **$550-$675**

Author's Collection

A Schreiner Look-alike

by Jarin Kasi

This outstanding brooch very closely replicates one of Schreiner of New York's most enduringly popular collectible designs – the "ruffle" brooch. Using keystone rhinestones like those specially ordered by Schreiner for the vintage originals, a ruffle of sorts is formed by layering the stones along the edges of the oversized brooch. The back construction of this Jarin Kasi piece is very close to how the Schreiner originals were made in a variety of colors.

The main difference between the old and new versions is that the Jarin piece is made of sterling silver and marked Jarin Sterling. Jarin Kasi is a California-based jewelry designer frequently inspired by vintage jewelry, although not all of his designs mimic originals as closely as this one.

Schreiner brooch set, c. 1950s, large royal blue rhinestones and purple cabochons with lavender and purple round and baguette accents in gunmetal settings, unmarked, domed brooch 2 5/8" wide, earrings 1 1/4". **$275-$325**

Author's Collection

BELOW Schreiner poodle brooch, c. 1950s, light brown and yellow rhinestones with red nose in gunmetal setting, marked Schreiner New York, 1 7/8" wide. **$150-$200**

Author's Collection

FAR LEFT Schreiner necklace/ pendant, c. 1960s, art glass cabochons with slate blue and pale pink inverted rhinestones in coppery setting, can be detached from matching chain and worn as a brooch, marked Schreiner New York, adjusts to 20 1/2" long, brooch/ pendant 2 3/4" long. **$325-$400**

Author's Collection

LEFT Schreiner adjustable ring, c. 1950s, large oval simulated turquoise art glass cabochon surrounded by emerald-cut brown rhinestones, marked "Schreiner New York" on the back, 1 3/4" long. **$175-$225**

Author's Collection

STANLEY HAGLER, MARK MERCY, AND IAN ST. GIELAR

DESIGNERS AND MANUFACTURERS

Stanley Hagler began designing and crafting jewelry in the 1950s. His hand-manipulated works comprised of simulated pearls and Swarovski rhinestones are desirable collectibles today. He crafted many other styles of jewelry as well, including Art Deco-inspired pieces using glass and acrylic resin components in the 1960s. He signed his jewelry

RIGHT Ian St. Gielar necklace set, c. mid-2000s, large molded black glass floral element surrounded by black seed beads, rose montee rhinestones, and faux pearl accents with matching earrings, marked Stanley Hagler N.Y.C. and Ian St. Gielar. **$525-600**

Jewelry courtesy ChicAntiques.com

BELOW Ian St. Gielar brooch, c. mid-2000s, large mother of pearl elements surrounded by gold-tone leaf and flower findings, black seed beads and faux pearl accents, marked Stanley Hagler N.Y.C. and Ian St. Gielar. **$275-$325**

Jewelry courtesy ChicAntiques.com

Stanley Hagler with a cartouche similar to that of Miriam Haskell until the early 1980s when he moved to Florida and his brand reportedly changed to Stanley Hagler N.Y.C. He worked alone until the early 1990s.

The truth about most Stanley Hagler jewelry being marketed today, including pieces shown in a number of well-known reference guides on costume jewelry, is that it wasn't made by Stanley Hagler or even under his direction. These pieces, which are gorgeous and collectible in their own right, were crafted by either Ian St. Gielar prior to his death in 2007, Gielar's widow, Valentina, since Ian's death, or Mark Mercy, who is also still in business.

Both St. Gielar and Mercy worked in Stanley Hagler's workshop before he died in 1996. After Hagler's death, both men continued using his name on jewelry, claiming they had the right to do so. So what's the real story about who should carry on the Hagler tradition?

Hagler's brother reportedly sided with Mercy over St. Gielar in

Stanley Hagler brooch, c. 1980s, floral motif comprised of seed pearls with faceted and rose montee rhinestone accents and antique gold-tone leaf findings on filigree backing, marked Stanley Hagler N.Y.C., 3 1/2" wide. **$425-$500**

Jewelry courtesy ChicAntiques.com

Mark Mercy brooch, c. early 2000s, gold-tone flower and basket findings with multicolor seed bead and faux pearl flowers and leaves, marked M&M Designs Fla, 2 1/2" long. **$175-$225**

Jewelry courtesy ChicAntiques.com

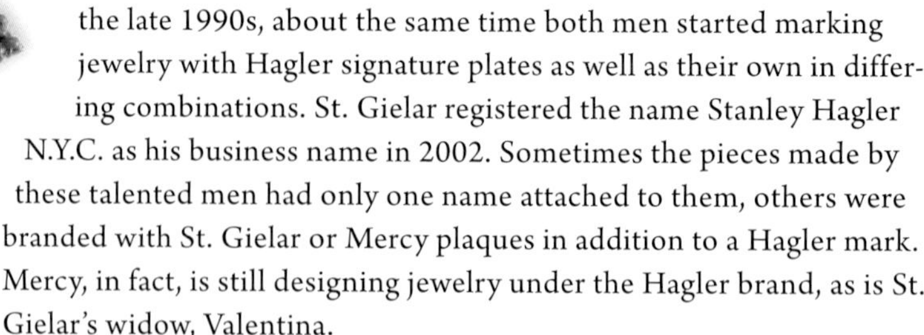

the late 1990s, about the same time both men started marking jewelry with Hagler signature plates as well as their own in differing combinations. St. Gielar registered the name Stanley Hagler N.Y.C. as his business name in 2002. Sometimes the pieces made by these talented men had only one name attached to them, others were branded with St. Gielar or Mercy plaques in addition to a Hagler mark. Mercy, in fact, is still designing jewelry under the Hagler brand, as is St. Gielar's widow, Valentina.

With such controversy surrounding the saga, we may never know whom Hagler intended as his successor, and identifying Hagler pieces and who made them, obviously and unfortunately, is mucked up by all this mixing and mingling of marks. But it's safe to say that if you have a piece marked Stanley Hagler N.Y.C. and it is big, bold and colorful, it's more than likely a post-1996 piece made after Hagler's death.

MARKS ON HAGLER, MERCY, AND ST. GIELAR JEWELRY

FIGURE 1

FIGURE 2

FIGURE 3

FIGURE 4

A number of different marks have been used on both pre-1996 Stanley Hagler pieces and those produced by Mark Mercy and the St. Gielar workshop dating after Mr. Hagler's death. There are a few subtle differences to note when identifying and dating this type of jewelry.

Stanley Hagler FIGURE 1

This mark was found on an older pearl piece made pre-1996 by the original Hagler workshop. Notice the spacing and shape of the C in N.Y.C. are slightly different from those shown on newer marks. Another older mark (not shown) looks very much like the oval cartouche used by Miriam Haskell with, of course, the Stanley Hagler name.

Mark Mercy FIGURES 2 & 3

Former Hagler designer Mark Mercy has used this version of the Stanley Hagler N.Y.C. mark on his recent work. He has also been known to use the M&M Designs Fla. mark shown here on jewelry made in the late 1990s and early 2000s.

Ian St. Gielar FIGURE 4

Many pieces made by former Hagler designer Ian St. Gielar in the late 1990s were marked Stanley Hagler N.Y.C (without a period behind the C) to distinguish it, somewhat, from pre-1996 Hagler. Later pieces were marked as shown with both plaques, but they can also be labeled with just the St. Gielar mark.

Mark Mercy necklace, c. 2012, art glass cabochon surrounded with seed beads, faceted pearls, and rhinestones in pale pink, lavender, and amethyst purple, 18" long with 7" center element including dangles, marked Stanley Hagler N.Y.C. **$400-$475**

Jewelry courtesy ChicAntiques.com

BELOW Ian St. Gielar brooch, c. mid-2000s, coral, vivid blue, spring green, and a touch of white in glass elements and seed beads, marked Stanley Hagler N.Y.C. and Ian St. Gielar, 3 7/8" long. **$275-$325**

Jewelry courtesy ChicAntiques.com

RIGHT Mark Mercy Christmas tree brooch, c. 2012, gold-tone basket base with green glass beads and faux seed pearls, along with red and aurora borealis accent rhinestones, marked Stanley Hagler N.Y.C, 3 3/4" long. **$250-$325**

Jewelry courtesy ChicAntiques.com

Mark Mercy necklace set, c. early 2000s, yellow beads with yellow seed beads and clear rhinestone accents on gold-tone backings, purchased directly from Mark Mercy, marked Stanley Hagler N.Y.C., necklace 19 1/2" long with each front section 1 5/8", earrings 3/4" wide. **$225-$250**

Author's Collection

TRIFARI

DESIGNERS AND MANUFACTURERS

With Coro, Trifari is one of the "big two" in American costume jewelry production. The earliest Trifari pieces are marked KTF (with the T larger than K and F) for Trifari, Kushman, and Fishel – the three men who operated this legendary Rhode Island jewelry business. The company used this mark from 1935, when it was first registered, through the end of 1937. Some of the finest pieces made by Trifari have this mark, and many of them emulate fine jewelry in fabulous Art Deco styles.

In fact, the rare emerald and rhinestone bracelet shown here is an exact copy of a Van Cleef & Arpels design featured in a *Life Magazine* spread on

LEFT *Life Magazine* illustration from article on "Junk Jewelry."

Courtesy Robin Deutsch Collection

KTF emerald shield-shaped dress clip, c. 1937, complementary piece to the KTF bracelet shown here, fastens with dress clip mechanism, marked KTF and number 78 for the stonesetter, 1 7/8" x 1 7/8". **$775-$975**

Jewelry courtesy Robin Deutsch Collection

KTF bracelet, c. 1937, rhodium-plated base metal, prong-set emerald-cut faux emeralds with bezel set rhinestones, channel-set baguettes and pavé-set round rhinestones, fold-over clasp integrated into the design, marked KTF, 1 1/4" wide, central element 3/4" high. **$5,000-$6,000**

Jewelry courtesy Robin Deutsch Collection

"Junk Jewelry" published in January 1938. It is exceedingly rare since these bracelets were all laboriously hand set, and it's unlikely that many were produced. Mimicking platinum and diamonds, they were made in four color schemes – all clear and clear with simulated emeralds, sapphires, or rubies. The same type of construction was used on the matching dress clip.

Trifari also did a remarkable job of copying Van Cleef & Arpels "mystery set" jewelry during the mid-1930s as exemplified by the exceptional ruby and clear rhinestone bracelet shown here. Collectors most often refer to these pieces as "invisibly" set. Rather than each simulated stone being calibré cut as with fine jewelry, however, they are actually comprised of strips of stones closely set together to achieve the same look. Ten ruby-colored strips were employed to make this bracelet. A number of these Art Deco designs were etched with a stone setter's mark in addition to the KTF branding. Many fine jewelers, including designers, model makers, and stone setters, worked in the costume jewelry industry during the Great Depression, and they were consummate craftsmen.

In 1938, the name Trifari was trademarked and the company began using this mark on its jewelry. There are anomalies where a KTF-marked piece has been found with a patent number dating to 1939, and in certain cases the same model has been found marked both KTF and Trifari, manufactured at different times. Very rarely, both stamps have even been noted on the same piece during the transitional period, according to avid Trifari collector and jewelry historian Robin Deutsch.

Much attention, and rightly so, is devoted to lead designer Alfred Philippe, who worked for Trifari from 1930 through 1968. He is responsible for some of the company's most celebrated designs including its copies of Cartier's "Tutti Frutti" pieces now referenced as "fruit salad" by collectors. One thing to be aware of, however, is that like most big costume jewelry companies, Trifari employed a team of designers and likely used free-lancers as well. Not every piece of jewelry matching a patent submitted with Alfred Philippe's name on it was actually designed by the man himself. Philippe is known to have worked closely with Jean Paris and Andre Boeuf in the 1950s and 1960s, along with others throughout his career.

It's also interesting to note, in spite of reports to the contrary, that Carl Fishel – who served as Trifari's president – was never associated with the company that manufactured jewelry under the Fishel Nessler brand (learn more about Fishel Nessler and the details dispelling this rumor in the 1920s category in Section One of this book).

With very rare exception, especially after 1937, all Trifari jewelry was marked. The marked changed a bit over the decades, ranging from the early

BELOW KTF "invisibly" set faux ruby bracelet. c. 1936, made of rhodium-plated base metal with 10 bead-set rhinestone pavé links and channel-set baguettes running down the center, and invisibly set simulated rubies, the fully articulated links are slightly curved to mold to the wrist, fold-over clasp integrates into the design, marked KTF and 53 for the stonesetter, 7" long x 3/4" wide. **$1,650-$1,850**

Jewelry courtesy Robin Deutsch Collection

KTF mark to the latest, which is Trifari without a crown. Most jewelry from the 1940s through the early 1970s had a crown over the T; the presence of a crown doesn't indicate a higher-end line, but rather that a piece is not contemporary. More recent marks without a crown were first in a cursive script and then in a more blocked style. Reissues made in 1996 and thereafter have a TM for trademark after the block Trifari mark. Earlier jewelry and pieces made through much of the 1940s were finely crafted; most of the jewelry made thereafter is more of the mass-market type, albeit still of high quality.

In the 1970s both Diane Love and Kunio Matsumoto designed lines for Trifari. The pieces based on ancient artifacts envisioned by Love were marked with paper hangtags, indicating they were her designs, although the jewelry itself was marked Trifari. Matsumoto's pieces were clearly marked with the designer's signature as well as the Trifari brand. Other notable designers who did work for Trifari were Kenneth Jay Lane in the 1970s and Bennetto Panetta in the early 1940s.

Trifari jewelry produced from 1942-1947 was made of sterling silver, and many pieces had a gold wash. Many of the company's whimsical "jelly belly" designs were finely crafted of sterling silver. These figural pieces were made using acrylic resin, also known as Lucite, from leftover airplane windows. The plastic panes were flawed and not suitable for aircraft manufacture, but they could certainly be salvaged for jewelry at a time when viable materials were scarce. Former Trifari CEO Irving Wolfe, who joined the company in 1940, confirmed this fact in a speech given at a jewelry collectors convention in the early 2000s. Master of modern design Norman Bel Geddes was commissioned to do a jelly belly sailfish pin clip for Trifari in the early 1940s. This is one of the designs that Trifari reissued in 1996 as part of its classics collection.

Clip-mates were Trifari's version of the "Duette" patented by Coro in the early 1930s (see "Coro" for Duette examples). These are usually marked Clip-mates on the clips themselves. Versions made in 1936 and 1937 may also have the KTF mark, although some early examples only have a patent number. Those made after 1937 are marked Trifari, and some pieces may have a stone setter's mark. Trifari also made bracelets that could accommodate clips when they were removed from the standard Clip-mates brooch mechanism.

Trifari advertising from the late 1940s into the 1950s shows many matching necklace, bracelet, and earring sets in colored rhinestones for day and

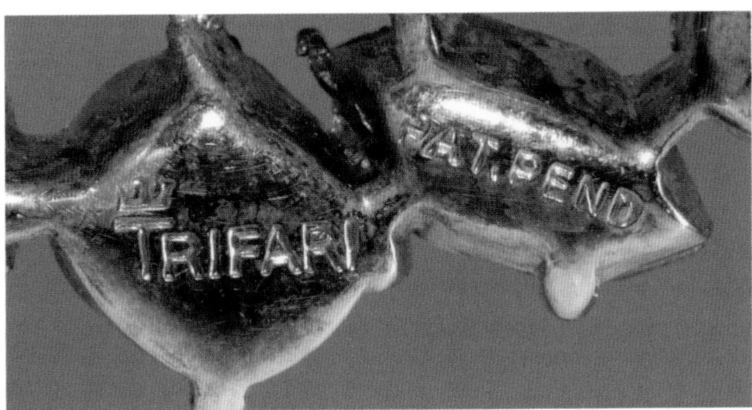

clear rhinestones for evening. These were widely advertised as gift ideas and sold well. They wore quite well, too, so there are many available for collectors to purchase at reasonable prices today. In 1953, Trifari introduced a line of British-inspired jewelry featuring crowns and scepters to commemorate Queen Elizabeth's coronation. These were different designs compared to earlier sterling silver Trifari crowns that sold so well in the 1940s.

Trifari followed fashion trends from the 1960s through the 1980s. The company made many designs with brushed gold-tone finishes along with faux pearl and simulated turquoise embellishments in the early 1960s, and then fun figurals in the mid-'60s. The Jewels of India collections in jewel tones introduced in 1965 and related L'Oriente styles in updated colors that include white enameling are all popular with collectors today. The brushed gold-tone figural pins, including many dog breeds, made in the mid-1960s also have a following. In the early 1970s Trifari made bold gold-tone jewelry including intriguing cuff bracelets. In the mid-1980s the company used enamels in various colors in competition with other companies that were mass-marketing jewelry for sale in department stores.

In the mid-1990s, Trifari reissued some of its classic styles. The newer pieces look a bit different in terms of the components used and, much to the joy of collectors, they are also marked with the date so they aren't confused with older production.

Trifari baton brooch, c. 1950, patented design featuring gold-plated metal with articulated tassels, 3 3/8" long. **$50-$75**

Jewelry courtesy ChicAntiques.com

BELOW Trifari basket brooch, c. 1950s, red and clear rhinestones in oval and round shapes, marked Trifari, 2 5/8" wide. **$200-$250**

Jewelry courtesy LinsyJsJewels.com

Trifari cross brooch, c. 1996, royal blue, ruby red, and emerald green cabochons with clear accents on polished gold-tone metal, reissue of a vintage design as part of a classics series marketed by Trifari in 1996, 2 3/4" long. **$100-$135**

Jewelry courtesy ChicAntiques.com

Trifari eagle brooch, c. early 1940s, rhodium-plated with pavé-set clear rhinestones and enameled accents, marked Trifari, wings 3 3/8" wide. **$450-$600**

Jewelry courtesy LinsyJsJewels.com

Trifari fruit salad necklace, c. early 1940s, opalescent molded fruits with tiny ruby red glass cabochons and clear accents, 16" long, marked Trifari. **$275-$350**

Jewelry courtesy LinsyJsJewels.com

ABOVE Trifari bracelet, c. late 1950s, red rhinestones and simulated pearls in rhodium-plated metal, marked Trifari, 7" long x 1" wide. **$400-$550**

Jewelry courtesy LinsyJsJewels.com

LEFT Trifari fur clip, c. early 1940s, red and light blue moonstone cabochons with clear rhinestones, brown enameling on some stems, original stones, marked Trifari, 3 3/4". **$350-$425**

Jewelry courtesy LinsyJsJewels.com

Trifari brooch set, c. 1960s, brushed gold-tone metal with ruby red rhinestones and simulated pearls, marked Trifari, brooch 1 3/4". **$150-$200**

Jewelry courtesy LinsyJsJewels.com

Trifari brooch set, c. 1960s, brushed gold-tone metal with simulated lapis stones and clear rhinestone accents, marked Trifari, brooch 2 1/2", earrings 1" wide. **$125-$165**

Jewelry courtesy LinsyJsJewels.com

Trifari necklace, c. late 1960s, simulated jade resin with gold-tone Chinese coins, Buddha figurals and dangling pagodas, marked Trifari, 16 3/4" long, central dangle just under 5" long, dangles at the sides 2 1/4" long. **$175-$225**

Jewelry courtesy ChicAntiques.com

Trifari dachshund brooch, c. mid-1960s, brushed gold-tone metal, 1 7/8" long. **$65-$85**

Jewelry courtesy ChicAntiques.com

WEISS

DESIGNERS AND MANUFACTURERS

It's said that Albert Weiss, who founded his jewelry company in 1942, never manufactured any of the jewelry branded with his famous name. This was confirmed by employees who worked for jobbers producing jewelry stamped Weiss. But a newspaper article from the *Toledo Blade* shows Walter deCremieux, who was a designer for Weiss, hand-painting metal flower jewelry to give to customers during an in-store promotional visit in the spring of 1968.

So what are collectors to make of this? Well, first, it doesn't really confirm that Weiss manufactured jewelry even if employees were responsible for decorating white "blanks" of some of the enameled flower pins popular during the late 1960s. According to the article, Weiss had an art department, and deCremieux worked his way up through the ranks starting as a stock boy with aspirations to become a designer. Once he reached his goal, he sketched designs and made models, just as his contemporaries working for other firms were doing at that time. The article never mentions the actual production of the "nature-inspired" creations deCremieux was responsible for designing, other than the hand painting that went on in the store on that particular day.

As for the aforementioned jewelry purchased from a manufacturer with his name affixed, these were the styles of the 1950s Weiss had in common with Eisenberg. This has been confirmed by employees who manufactured the jewelry, but were most certainly not working directly for Weiss. Many pieces made in these styles used rich gray rhinestones in a hue akin to gray quartz. These pieces were widely advertised as "Black Diamond by Albert Weiss." They weren't exclusives, however. A limited number of these pieces can be found with the Eisenberg mark as well.

Another piece of advertising from 1956 mentions pieces "expertly crafted by famous Albert Weiss." While that doesn't appear to be the case, given what we know about the company thus far, the hand-pronged settings, non-tarnishable rhodium backs, and a dazzling selection of earrings, pins, necklaces, and

bracelets in 14 colors mentioned in the ad can't be disputed. Not all Weiss jewelry made after 1955 was marked with a © symbol, so using vintage advertising widely searchable online is a great way to date these pieces.

If nothing else, Weiss was an avid marketer, and a successful one to boot. Many pieces of his jewelry are available to collectors today, and the top-of-the-line styles sell for good sums. These include his "India inspired" pieces appearing in *Vogue* in 1960 and larger clear rhinestone or colored necklaces. Weiss Christmas tree pins that sold for $3 apiece in 1963 are also avidly sought by collectors of that type of jewelry as well.

It's also prudent to keep in mind that Weiss and Hobé reproductions were coming out of Rhode Island in the mid-2000s. Many of these "fantasies," or counterfeits, look nothing like the jewelry collectors usually associate with Weiss, or Hobé for that matter. Many were sold for bargain prices on eBay, and they're now being passed from hand to hand as genuine articles by unknowing sellers. Shrewd collectors do their homework regarding valid Weiss styles by reviewing vintage advertising online to avoid being fooled by these fakes.

RIGHT Weiss brooch, c. 1960, from the India Inspired collection, sapphire blue rock-shaped specialty stone surrounded by teal green, peacock blue, and royal blue rhinestones, setting is antiqued silver-tone metal, marked Weiss, 2 1/4" long. **$125-$175**

Courtesy of ChicAntiques.com

FAR RIGHT Weiss crown pin, c. 1950s, blue and red glass cabochons, red and clear rhinestones, and simulated pearls set in antiqued gold-tone metal, marked Weiss, 1 7/8" wide. **$150-$200**

Jewelry courtesy LinsyJsJewels.com

Weiss brooch set, c. 1950s, gray "Black Diamond" rhinestones with clear accents in rhodium-plated metal work, marked Weiss on each piece, brooch 2 1/8" diameter, earrings 1". **$125-$175**

Jewelry courtesy LinsyJsJewels.com

Weiss brooch set, c. 1960s, brown and olive green elongated navettes with aurora borealis accents in antiqued silver-tone setting, marked Weiss on all pieces, brooch 2 1/4" diameter, earrings 7/8". **$175-$225**

Jewelry courtesy LinsyJsJewels.com

Weiss bracelet set, c. 1950s, red rhinestones with clear accents in rhodium-plated metal work, marked Weiss on each piece, bracelet 7", brooch 2 3/8" diameter, earrings 1 1/4". **$225-$300**

Jewelry courtesy LinsyJsJewels.com

BELOW Weiss shield brooch, c. early 1960s, sapphire blue specialty stone surrounded by sapphire blue and aurora borealis rhinestones in gunmetal setting, marked Weiss, 2 3/4" long. **$125-$175**

Jewelry courtesy LinsyJsJewels.com

LEFT Weiss brooch set, c. late 1950s, ice blue, sapphire blue, and aurora borealis rhinestones in silver-tone setting, marked Weiss on each piece, brooch 3" diameter, earrings 1 1/2". **$200-$250**

Jewelry courtesy LinsyJsJewels.com

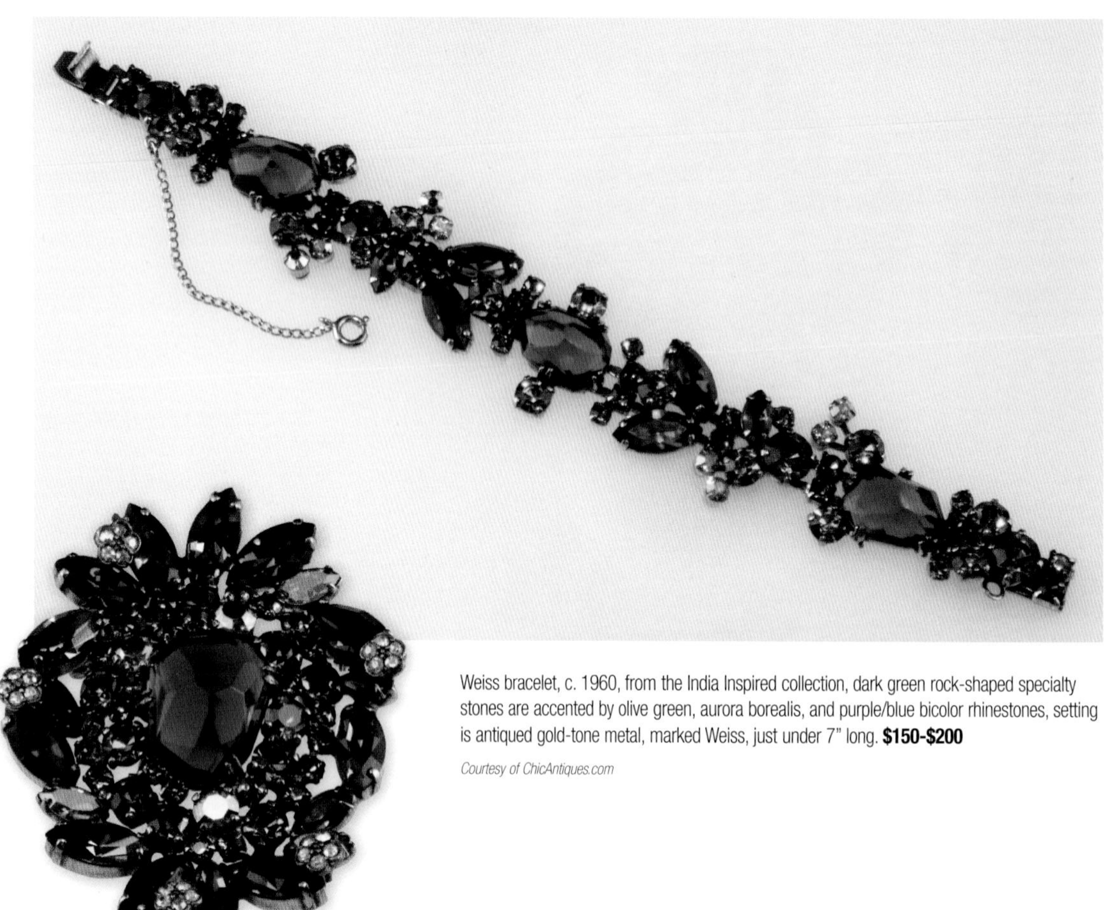

Weiss bracelet, c. 1960, from the India Inspired collection, dark green rock-shaped specialty stones are accented by olive green, aurora borealis, and purple/blue bicolor rhinestones, setting is antiqued gold-tone metal, marked Weiss, just under 7" long. **$150-$200**

Courtesy of ChicAntiques.com

ABOVE Weiss brooch, c. 1960, from the India Inspired collection, dark green rock-shaped specialty stone surrounded by olive green, aurora borealis, and purple/blue bicolor rhinestones, setting is antiqued gold-tone metal, marked Weiss, 2 1/4" long. **$125-$175**

Courtesy of ChicAntiques.com

Weiss necklace, c. 1950s, clear brilliantly faceted rhinestones in silver-tone metal, marked Weiss, adjusts to 16" long. **$75-$125**

Courtesy of ChicAntiques.com

SUPPLEMENTAL MARKS GUIDE

DESIGNERS AND MANUFACTURERS

Keep in mind that circa dating jewelry based solely on the mark on a piece sometimes can be precise and other times quite misleading. A number of companies used various marks, and they reused the same or very similar marks over many decades. Ciner, Miriam Haskell, and Napier are a few examples of the manufacturers employing this practice.

As a general rule, however, marks that include a © symbol (for copyright) mean the piece was made after the mid-1950s. Determining how far after the 1950s that manufacture occurred takes a bit more detective work. Be sure to look at the overall design, components, and construction techniques in addition to consulting marks guides when dating your collectible costume jewelry.

Many of the following marks relate to jewelry shown in Section One of this guide.

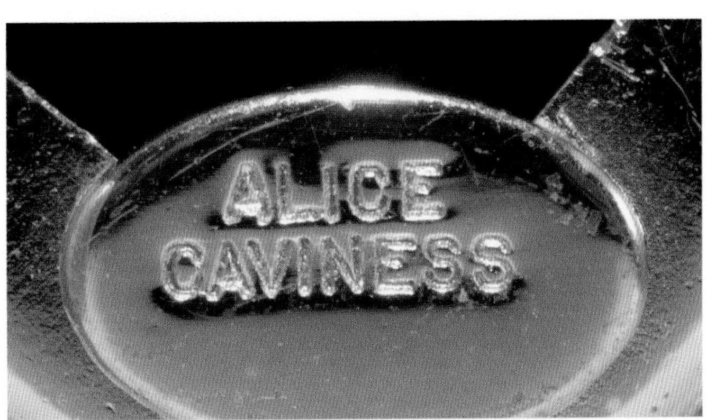

ALICE CAVINESS

In business 1945 to late 1990s (mark shown 1950-1960s)

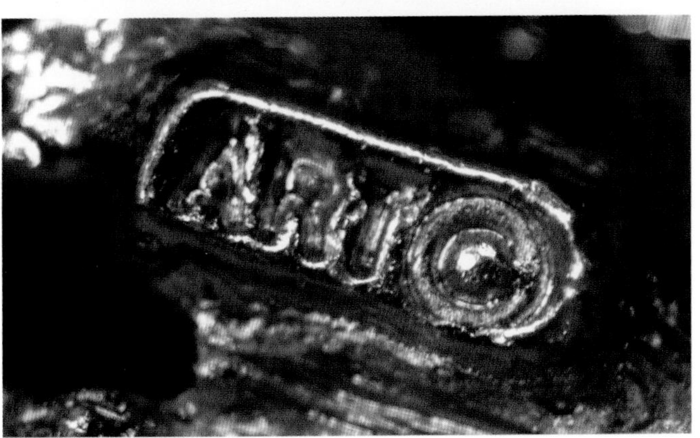

ART

Mark of ModeArt, in business early 1950s to 1980 (mark shown 1960s)

BAUER

Dorothy Bauer, in business 1982 to 2007 (mark shown 1990s)

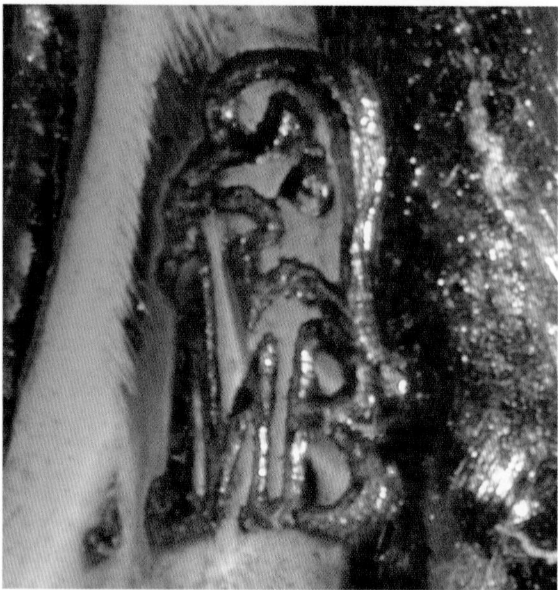

BOUCHER MB

1937-1949, and rarely until 1955 (mark shown 1940s)

BOUCHER

1950-1954 without ©, after 1955 with © (mark shown 1960s)

CASTLECLIFF

In business 1918-1977; first marked jewelry 1941 (mark shown 1960s)

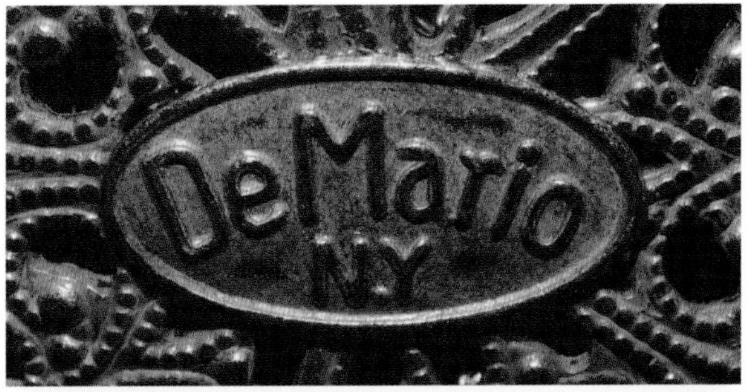

DE MARIO NY

Robert DeMario in business 1945-1965 (mark shown 1950s)

FLORENZA

1940s to 1981 (mark shown late 1950s)

©HOLLYCRAFT

Used by Hollywood Jewelry 1960-1971

HOLLYCRAFT

Used by Hollywood Jewelry on 1950s lines

J.J.

Mark of Jonette Jewelry used 1943 to 2006 (mark shown 1960s)

MARVELLA

1911 to present
(mark shown 1950s)

MIMI DI N

Mark of Mimi di Nascemi from 1962 to mid-1980s (mark shown 1960s)

MONET JEWELERS

1937 to mid-1940s (mark shown late 1930s)

MONET

late 1950s-1970s (mark shown 1960s)

MONOCRAFT

Forerunner to Monet; used on mid-1930s monogram jewelry

ORIGINAL BY ROBÉRT

In business 1942 to 1975 (mark shown 1950s-1960s)

REBAJES

Mark of Frank Rebajes used 1930s-1950s

REGENCY & REGENCY JEWELS (REGINA NOVELTY CO.)

1940s to 1972 (mark shown 1950s)

RENOIR/MATISSE

Renoir mark 1946-1964, Matisse added to enameled lines after 1952

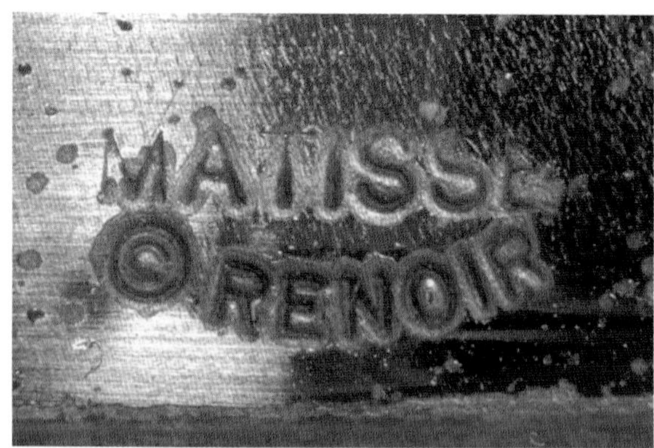

SCHAUER OF NEW YORK

Mark used on 1950s-1960s jewelry

SHERMAN

Canadian company in business 1947 to 1981 (mark shown late 1950s-1960s)

STARET

Used by Chicago-based Staret Jewelry Co. from 1941-1947

SWAROVSKI

Jewelry made 1977 to present; swan mark first used in 1988

TRIGÉRE

First used 1960 by Pauline Trigére

WHITING & DAVIS

1926 to 1991 for jewelry (mark shown 1970s)

WM. DE LILLO

William de Lillo and Robert Clark dating 1967 to mid-1970s

For many more marks examples and dating information, visit Researching Costume Jewelry at *www.illusionjewels.com.*

Section Three

DATING AND IDENTIFYING COSTUME JEWELRY

Accurately dating and identifying collectible costume jewelry comes with study and experience, and also with not believing everything you read in marketing descriptions. Regardless of the style, a piece of jewelry with iridescent aurora borealis stones wasn't made in the 1930s. No matter how "vintage" a piece looks, if it's marked with a contemporary company name – like Loren Bell, Pierre Lorion Sylvia Karels, or Jarin Kasi, among many others listed in the "Contemporary" category in Section One of this book – it was made within the past 10-15 years. And not every piece of unsigned jewelry can accurately be attributed to a maker.

When avid collectors and dealers are shopping for jewelry in the field, one of the first things they do when they pick up a piece is look at the back. The obvious notion is that they're looking for a mark of some sort to determine which company made the item, or where it originated in the world, and that's true. But that's not all they're trying to find out. Even when jewelry isn't marked, clues can be found regarding its origin and when it was made, by examining the sum of the parts. And sometimes the skeleton discovered by looking at the back will tell more about the piece than its pretty face in terms of quality and potential value.

That's not to say that a beautiful piece of unsigned jewelry can't stand on its own merit. It can, indeed. But being able to attribute a maker, when possible, and to accurately date and describe materials used in construction helps not only those selling vintage jewelry, but those who are shopping for pieces made by specific manufacturers or crafted during various periods. It also makes locating pieces made in distinctive styles or using unique components easy to find through online search engines when they are correctly described.

Many jewelry items are misattributed and/or misdated, however, so always take the "buyer beware" stance. This is especially true when approaching unsigned pieces. Learn as much as possible about specific manufacturers, styles, and components and you'll feel more confident in identifying, or confirming, the era when they were made and which company likely produced them.

And don't forget numerous vintage advertising pages and articles related to costume jewelry have been scanned and shared online. These can be very instrumental in dating vintage pieces with a bit of research. Patent information leading to precise dating for costume jewelry designs and components have also been widely researched and documented. Collections of patent sketches are available through many online and print-based resources including books written by Carla and Roberto Brunialti and Julia C. Carroll listed in the bibliography of this reference.

Identifying and Dating Jewelry by Examining Stones

While you can't always determine the age or origin of a piece of jewelry by simply looking at the stones used in the design (many contemporary designers use vintage stones in their artistry), it's a good place to start. Stones were introduced at different periods and they evolved over time, so paying close attention to cuts, the way they were molded, and colors can be helpful in narrowing down the age of a piece. It's also helpful (and quite fun!) at times when you're trying to determine the origin of a piece to be a bit of a stone detective.

AURORA BOREALIS

Swarovski didn't make the popular iridescent rhinestones known as aurora borealis until 1955, so vintage pieces containing them in any coloration will not predate the mid-1950s. They have been used prolifically in

Sherman aurora borealis set, c. late 1950s, similar in design and construction to Schreiner. Completely crafted with aurora borealis rhinestones in gold-tone settings, marked Sherman. **$225-$250**

Jewelry courtesy of ChicAntiques.com

Blue aurora borealis bib necklace, c. late 1950s, completely set with blue aurora borealis rhinestones in silver-tone setting, unmarked.
$125-$150

Jewelry courtesy of ChicAntiques.com

jewelry since then, however.

Not all pieces containing aurora borealis stones are old. New jewelry, including imports from China and elsewhere, can be found with aurora borealis stones, some of which don't measure up to Swarovski quality. Looking for other clues, such as the style and construction of a piece as well as manufacturer's marks, are also important when dating aurora borealis jewelry.

Keep in mind that iridescent beads and crystals were used earlier, especially in the 1930s. Usually described as "carnival" finish rather than aurora borealis, they're oftentimes larger in size and have a lighter coating of iridescence than more modern beads used in the 1950s and 1960s.

FOILED CABOCHONS OR "CAT'S EYE"

Various types of foiled cabochons have been used in jewelry manufacture over the decades, and those nicknamed "cat's eye" by collectors were placed in designs by many different manufacturers from the mid-1950s through the 1960s. Some contemporary designers use these vintage stones today, when they can find them.

There are also different types of foiled cabochons, which are essentially domed pieces of glass with foil applied to the back to give them an art glass effect. DeLizza & Elster, Regency, and Austrian pieces can all be found with these stones beautifully decorating them. In fact, nearly every popular jewelry manufacturer from Coro to Kramer to Weiss made some type of jewelry featuring these mesmerizing specialty stones.

Coro foiled cabochon brooch, c. early 1960s, center foiled cabochon surrounded by aurora borealis rhinestones.
$45-$55

Jewelry courtesy of ChicAntiques.com

Foiled cabochon detail in Kramer bracelet, c. 1950s. See Kramer in Section Two to view full piece.

Foiled cabochon detail in Regency bracelet, c. 1950s. See 1950s in Section One to view full piece.

FRUIT SALAD

Fruit salad stones were first copied after Cartier "Tutti Frutti" fine jewelry made with carved rubies, sapphires, and emeralds in the late 1920s and early 1930s. These precious gems were shaped like small fruits, such as lemons, apples, and pears, along with leaves. What costume jewelry collectors term as fruit salad are pieces made with molded glass to resemble the same styles of fruits and leaves. Early pieces by Trifari offer prime examples, and they are very desirable to collectors.

When used in costume jewelry, the colors can vary widely, so it's the shape of the stones rather than the color that indicates a fruit salad piece. Items made in the 1930s and 1940s often have traditional jewel-tone colors like the fine jewelry originals they mimic. Some pastels, bright colors, and white fruit salad stones are also found decorating mid-century pieces.

These are also erroneously described as carved glass from time to time. They are indeed molded glass.

LEFT Fruit salad detail in Trifari necklace, c. 1940s. See Trifari in Section Two to view full piece.

GRIPOIX GLASS

First, be aware that many types of glass stones are misidentified as Gripoix. They are most often simply glass cabochons. The origin of these components is usually unknown, and sellers are using the term Gripoix generically, and incorrectly, to describe them. By and large, Gripoix glass was not used in the run-of-the-mill mass-produced costume jewelry of yesteryear, and it's not used in that type of jewelry today.

Glass beads, cabochons, coated pearls, and other components made by the House of Gripoix will be found in jewelry made by Chanel, Dior, Balenciaga, Givenchy, Isabel Canovas, and Pierre Cardin along with other European couture houses. A limited amount of jewelry also bears the Gripoix name.

Glass poured directly into a setting is usually evident when examining the back. (See "Poured Glass Vs. Molded Glass" in this section for an example of Gripoix poured glass.) Cabochon stones and beads made of Gripoix glass usually have slight nuances from stone to stone, as noted in the example shown here.

Gripoix glass and pearl brooch, c. mid-2000s; center stone, cranberry glass elements, and glass-coated pearls all made by the House of Gripoix, marked Gripoix Paris, 3 1/4" wide.
$1,200-$1,350

Jewelry courtesy of ChicAntiques.com

It was too expensive, and still is, to use this type of handcrafted French glass in lower quality jewelry, but many molded glass imitations were used in less expensive, non-couture pieces.

If you find a piece of intricately crafted jewelry incorporating genuine poured or finely blown glass components in the design, it's well worth looking into the origin and having the piece professionally evaluated by a costume jewelry expert (rather than a fine jeweler). Older pieces containing Gripoix glass are extremely valuable.

Coro sterling jelly belly fur clip, c. 1944, patented beetle pin clip with sapphire blue glass bullet cabochon eyes and Lucite back embellished with rhinestones. These were sold in pairs as "Twinkling Twins" or as part of a Duette. Marked Coro and Sterling, 1 1/2" wide.
$100-$150 single clip

Jewelry courtesy of ChicAntiques.com

JELLY BELLY CABOCHONS

Imagine the surprise of jewelry collectors attending a convention in the early 2000s when a former Trifari executive indicated that the clear acrylic resin used in their "Jelly Belly" jewelry from the 1940s was made using airplane window rejects. Not those coming home severely damaged after battle, mind you, but those that never made it to the front in the first place. These flawed pieces that were not suitable for an entire windshield were certainly viable when cut into smaller pieces, carved into domed shapes, polished to a high gloss, and mounted into the bellies of sterling silver costume jewelry figurals. At a time when jewelry-crafting components were in severely short supply, this repurposing of material made perfect sense.

Trifari wasn't the only jewelry company to make jelly belly – the collector's name for jewelry made with clear plastic mounted into figural pieces in a menagerie of styles – but its designs are some of the most well-known and desirable. Collectors also look for Coro and Corocraft designs with clear plastic bellies and unmarked examples as well. Pieces made after World War II can also be found made of plated base metals rather than plain or gold-washed sterling.

One thing new collectors and sellers sometimes get wrong is referencing glass or colored plastic cabochons as jelly bellies. To be a true jelly belly, the center area of the piece must be clear and made of Lucite, a trade name for acrylic resin.

Margarita stone, c. 1960s.

MARGARITA

The name of the decorative margarita stone refers to its shape rather than color. They are scalloped flower-shaped stones with holes in the center to sometimes accommodate a rhinestone-topped pin to hold them in place. Margaritas were popular in jewelry design beginning in the late 1950s and continuing into the 1960s. Collectors referenced them as "marguerite" stones for many years, but original vintage packaging has confirmed the name as margarita.

Margarita stones were manufactured by Swarovski in a number of bicolor and solid variations, including what collectors refer to as "watermelon" with pink in the center and green around the edge. Many manufacturers used them, including DeLizza & Elster in some of its most popular lines. Vendôme necklaces and other pieces were also crafted using margarita stones in clustered designs.

Vendôme margarita necklace set, c. 1960s, "Watermelon" or Vitrail Medium II stone clusters with light brown crystal beads and matching earrings, marked Vendôme, necklace adjusts from about 16 1/4" to 18" long. **$165-$185**

Jewelry courtesy of ChicAntiques.com

MEXICAN OPAL GLASS OR "DRAGON'S BREATH"

While some collectors and jewelry historians are adamantly against adopting nicknames for stones and jewelry styles in general, it happens nonetheless when clever collectors and enterprising marketers come into play. Thusly, Mexican opal glass stones have morphed into the more intriguing "Dragon's Breath" stones over the past decade or so.

These stones are made of glass mixed with metals to induce a bicolor effect ranging from red to blue, depending on how the light hits them, with an overall deep purplish cast. Those who reference them as Dragon's Breath see the flashes of color from within the stone as the "breath" from which the name is derived.

Stones like these were first used in jewelry in the early 1900s to simulate authentic fire or jelly opals. The older jewelry of this type is very often made of sterling silver and sometimes of Mexican origin. Older stones are most often transparent, unfoiled cabochons in round or oval shapes. It's also important to note some faceted examples were used in mid-century costume jewelry. This means you have to look at the overall style and construction for age clues when dating jewelry containing this type of stone.

Also be aware that these glass stones are often represented as jelly opals or fire opals in error as those are natural semi-precious gemstones rather than manufactured glass. Describing them as Mexican opal glass (as found on vintage packaging) as an alternative to Dragon's Breath is far less misleading.

Kramer brooch with Dragon's Breath stones, c. 1950s, marked Kramer, 2" wide. The round and pear-shaped cabochons, or stones with smooth rounded tops, in this brooch are referenced as "Dragon's Breath" by collectors. **$65-$85**

Jewelry courtesy of ChicAntiques.com

Unsigned earring, Dragon's Breath stone example, c. 1950s. The round and pear-shaped cabochons, or stones with smooth rounded tops, in this earring are referenced as "Dragon's Breath" by collectors.

POURED GLASS VS. MOLDED GLASS

Like the term Gripoix, poured glass is another term thrown around with abandon by jewelry marketers, and most of those attributions are incorrect.

ABOVE AND CENTER
Poured glass in Chanel jewelry, c. 1970s. Front and back examples of poured glass as seen in the 1970s Chanel Maltese cross pendant depicted in Section Two.

ABOVE, FAR RIGHT
Molded glass in metal findings, c. 1950s. These vintage molded glass petals in metal findings are similar to those used on Trifari jewelry from the 1950s. As shown in a Lawrence Vrba vase brooch featured in the 1990s examples in Section One.

What they're purporting as poured glass is actually molded glass like the metal-framed glass petals and flowers widely used by Trifari in the 1950s in both milk white and opaque colors. These have their own place in the history of collectible jewelry, but they're not poured glass pieces.

True poured glass was, and still is, literally achieved by pouring molten glass directly into a metal frame. These components can look a bit crudely made from the back, but the early pieces designed by the House of Chanel and other European couturiers from the 1930s through the 1960s are quite valuable and coveted, so learning to recognize them behooves the educated collector. Even newer poured glass couture pieces are quite popular and desirable.

RHINESTONES

Whether you call them rhinestones, paste, or diamantes (the latter two terms being more European in nature), sparkling jewels have been used to simulate diamonds and gemstones in costume jewelry for centuries now. Like diamonds and precious gems, rhinestones have a flat surface on the top called a "table." Looking at tables can be a great way to help confirm the date of jewelry when it comes to transitional pieces combining styles, or revival pieces that mimic older styles.

When examining stones in pieces from the late 1800s and early 1900s with a jeweler's loupe, you can see the difference. Rhinestone tables are smaller in diameter and the stones in general are taller in older costume jewelry. Newer round rhinestones have a shape more akin to the traditional shape of a round-cut diamond. Keep in mind, however, that sometimes old stock rhinestones were used in later production, so examining the other attributes of a piece is also necessary before surmising an age.

Another type of older rhinestone had multiple facets on the top and a flat back. These are indicative of the late 1800s through the 1920s, and were rarely used after that time.

You'll also note that many sellers use names for rhinestones that you may not be familiar with, such as navette for the marquis shape or chaton for round stones. Those are terms exclusive to rhinestones, while marquis and round cross over from fine to costume jewelry.

Glass stones have different origins as well, but most are Austrian (Swarovski), Czechoslovakian, or German in origin. Austrian rhinestones generally have more brilliance and less foil loss and discoloration over time in comparison to Czech and German stones. Of course, even Austrian rhine-

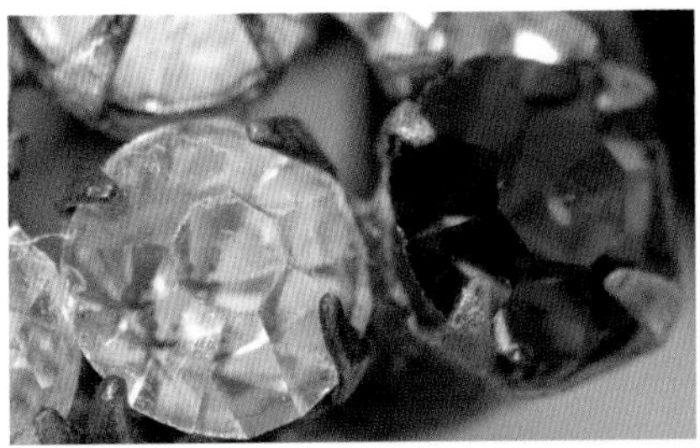

ABOVE, LEFT Victorian rhinestones, c. 1890s, as seen in a Victorian hatpin; the clear rhinestone is taller and has a smaller "table" when compared to newer examples.

ABOVE, CENTER Mid-century rhinestones, c. 1950s, photographed in a 1950s brooch; the blue stone's table is wider in comparison to old rhinestones.

ABOVE, RIGHT Domed faceted stones, c. late 1800s-early 1900s. These older stones have multiple facets on the top. They were used in round versions to simulate jet in the late 1800s and then in rhinestone versions later. As shown on an early 1900s E.A. Bliss brooch depicted in Section One.

stones stored in poor conditions, namely areas that are extremely hot, cold, or damp, can lose their sparkle.

Many older pieces of jewelry dating to the 1930s and earlier incorporate Czech stones in beautiful but odd colors that are sometimes harder to replace if one goes missing. This should be taken into consideration when repairs are being done. That goes for the aforementioned stones with higher/smaller tables found in older jewelry. In fact, it's better to look at these projects as restorations and make an effort to keep them as close to original as possible in order to maintain the integrity and value of the pieces.

RIVOLI

The rivoli is a type of multi-faceted foiled glass stone manufactured by Swarovski. They have flat backs and pointed tops. They were first used in costume jewelry in the 1950s and remained popular into the 1960s and beyond. DeLizza & Elster used rivolis in many of the company's most popular designs.

The name refers to the shape of the stone rather than the color, which can vary from bicolor examples to solid colors. Collectors sometimes refer to clear rivolis as "headlight" stones. These are usually prong-set but can also be glued in some settings.

Rivolis are usually rather large and prominent in designs, but sizes can vary. They are sometimes confused with inverted rhinestones such as those used in Schreiner jewelry from the 1950s and 1960s. See the unsigned Schreiner category in this section to view jewelry examples using inverted rhinestones for comparison.

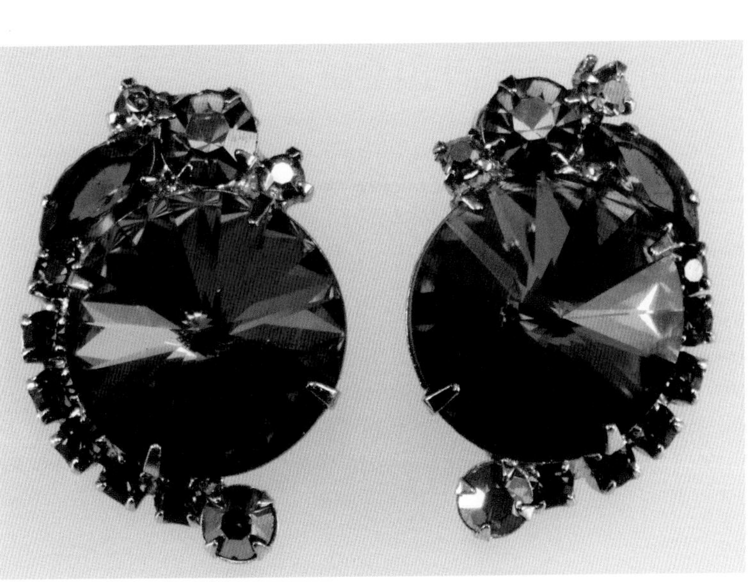

Juliana rivoli earrings, c. 1960s, unmarked. The large peacock blue center stones with flat backs and pointed tops are known as rivolis.
$55-$75

Jewelry courtesy of ChicAntiques.com

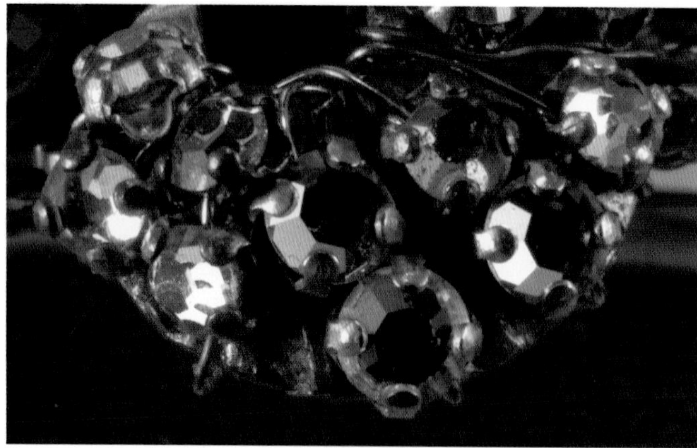

ABOVE Rose montee rhinestone detail on Miriam Haskell brooch, c. 1950s.

ABOVE, RIGHT Miriam Haskell brooch, c. 1950s, red unfoiled stones surrounded by clear rose montee rhinestones, marked Miriam Haskell, 2" long. **$300-$400**

Jewelry courtesy of LinsyJsJewels.com

ROSE MONTEE

Rose montees are small, flat-backed rhinestones with a mirror finish. Each stone is individually mounted into a metal-backed pronged setting, which lends to wiring or sewing these into place in jewelry design. They are most often clear although they surface in colors occasionally in vintage and more often in contemporary pieces.

Miriam Haskell used this type of stone prolifically clustered with pearls and other components in many designs made during the 1950s and 1960s. Other makers of similar styles like Robért, DeMario, and Eugene also used these stones. Contemporary designers and couture houses have used this type of rhinestone as well, for instance, fabric brooches with rhinestone embellishments made by Prada in 2004. They were, however, used in fashioning handmade fabric jewelry earlier too, so overall style and component factors must be considered when considering the presence of these stones in dating collectible jewelry.

Some jewelry guides refer to these as "roses" montees rather than rose montees. They are, however, marketed today as rose montee by stone distributors.

SAPHIRET OR SAPPHARINE

While they were named sappharine long ago by stone manufacturers, the term "saphiret" is firmly entrenched in the collector's vernacular today to describe this type of stone with a blue-brown hue made by adding a small amount of gold to blue glass during production. Saphiret beads were also made using the same glass formula.

Saphirets were first used in Victorian jewelry, and those pieces will have a decidedly older look to them with smaller saphirets in more delicate settings. In costume jewelry made during the 1950s and early 1960s, saphirets are usually much larger, and the overall designs are bolder in comparison.

Most saphirets are cabochons with rounded tops, and Regency led the pack in terms of incorporating them into a number of different styles. Some faceted examples can be found as well in mid-20th century jewelry,

ABOVE, LEFT Saphiret brooch, c. 1950s, five round cabochon saphirets enhanced by champagne-colored rhinestones, unmarked. **$225-$250**

Jewelry courtesy of ChicAntiques.com

ABOVE, RIGHT Saphiret bead wrap bracelet, c. late 1950s, saphiret beads with aurora borealis rondelle spacers. **$250-$275**

Jewelry courtesy of ChicAntiques.com

but they're not as common. Unusual pieces containing these stones can be quite valuable. All saphiret jewelry is popular with collectors today.

"WATERMELON" OR VITRAIL MEDIUM II

The names "watermelon" and Vitrail Medium II refer to a stone color rather than a shape. Collectors have nicknamed this stone "watermelon" because the primary colors are pink in the center and green on the outer edge. The glass stone likely derived its nickname due to its similarity to a natural gemstone known as watermelon tourmaline. Vitrail II Medium is the manufacturer's name for this type of stone.

Watermelon stones were incorporated in many pieces dating to the 1950s and 1960s bearing the Schiaparelli mark as well as many signed Judy Lee (a home party company). Some pieces of Juliana jewelry made in the 1960s by DeLizza & Elster are embellished with these stones in different shapes. The color is often seen in round and oval shapes, but can also be found in emerald cut and margarita or rivoli stones as well.

Keep in mind that colors for these stones can vary depending on the manufacturer, since Swarovski made them as well as Czech and German manufacturers. Vintage examples found in original packaging also vary slightly in color from year to year, according to jewelry designer and vintage stone expert Katerina Musetti.

Schiaparelli "watermelon" earrings, c. 1950s, round "watermelon" or Vitrail Medium II rhinestones in rope settings. **$100-$125**

Jewelry courtesy of ChicAntiques.com

Dating Jewelry Using Components and Findings

Some components and findings (parts or materials used in making a piece of jewelry) have been used in jewelry production for a very long time. Knowing this makes it difficult to look at a clasp or type of closure and determine a definitive timeframe in jewelry production history correlating with the item you're evaluating.

Others, however, were used only for a short period, so you can get an idea of how old the piece is based on that one attribute, as well as examining the piece as a whole for confirmation. At the very least, you can usually determine when an element came into use and know the piece you're evaluating is no older than that.

Keep in mind that clasps, pin stems, and other components can be replaced over time. For instance, if you have a necklace with all the earmarks of the Edwardian era, age appropriate wear, and components used in construction during that period, but it closes with a lobster claw clasp, you're probably either dealing with a newly made reproduction or the clasp has been replaced. Each component should be evaluated individually.

BRACELET CLASPS

When looking at clasps, keep in mind that you can certainly generalize about which type was used when, but looking at the overall style of the piece is important before determining when a bracelet was made. Many clasps were used over and over through the decades once they came into production.

Early bracelet examples from the Victorian era used two-part push clasps, also known as box clasps. In the early 1900s spring ring closures were sometimes used on bracelets. Spring rings in the 1920s changed to include a nib that allowed for easier opening and closing.

Fold-over clasps were used sparingly in the 1930s and became more popular in the 1940s. They were used frequently thereafter with wider versions of these clasps dating to the 1950s and beyond. Toggle clasps were used sparingly in 1950s and 1960s jewelry, but more frequently going forward.

TWO-PART BRACELET CLASP: An example of a two-part clasp used on Victorian jewelry through jewelry made today, sometimes referenced as a box clasp. As shown on an early 1900s bracelet.

TWO-PART BRACELET CLASP

BOX CLASP VARIATION

SPRING RING CLASP

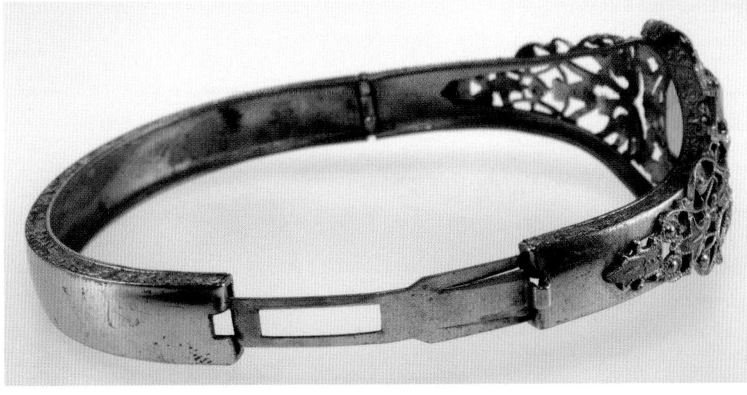
SLIDING CLASP

FOLD-OVER CLASP

TOGGLE CLASP

BOX CLASP VARIATION: This is a variation of the two-part clasp as seen on a 1930s bracelet.

SPRING RING CLASP: Used on jewelry from the 1920s through today. Earlier versions did not have the added nib to ease in opening the catch. As shown on a 1970s bracelet.

SLIDING CLASP: A version of this mechanism originated in Victorian hinged bangles. This example is on a 1920s bracelet.

FOLD-OVER CLASP: Used sparingly in the 1930s and 1940s, but from the 1950s on it has been popular in varied widths. As shown on a 1960s bracelet.

TOGGLE CLASP: Used sparingly in the 1950s and 1960s. Frequently used in modern jewelry with variations in size. As shown on a 1960s bracelet.

BROOCH AND PIN CLOSURES AND HINGES

The earliest brooch and pin closures were "C"-style clasps in several variations dating to the Victorian era. Safely clasps came about earlier in fine jewelry, but they were not widely used in costume jewelry design until 1915 or so. However, keep in mind that variations of the "C" clasp were used on inexpensive jewelry made during various periods. Most modern brooches are made with safety clasps, although occasionally "C" clasps will be found on inexpensive jewelry.

Trombone clasps were used on European jewelry largely from the 1890s through the 1940s. There are exceptions, though. Occasionally pieces with 1950s or 1960s attributes will be found with this type of clasp. Pierre Bex jewelry made from the 1960s through the 1980s used this clasp, as did other makers of revival styles during this period. Some Chanel brooches in the 1970s and 1980s also used very nice trombone clasps, so looking at the overall attributes of each piece is necessary in addition to recognizing this style.

Dress clips were produced in the 1920s in limited quantities and really surged in popularity in the 1930s. Double-pronged pin clip mechanisms, referred to as fur clips by collectors, were widely used in the 1930s and continued to be a popular pinning device during the 1940s.

Tube hinges were the earliest incorporated in brooches and pins. Ball hinges were first used in the 1890s. There is some overlap in use during the period, but by the early 1900s the ball hinge was primarily used. Various iterations have been used since then through modern production.

EARLY TUBE HINGE AND "C" CATCH: Tube hinge used on brooches primarily through the 1890s, although some early 1900s carryover designs have this finding. This style of "C" catch can be found on pieces through the early 1900s. As shown on the Victorian cameo depicted in Section One.

"C" CATCH: This style of "C" catch can be found on pieces from the late 1800s through the early 1900s, ranging from small bar pins to large sash pins. As shown on the Victorian tiger brooch depicted in Section One.

TROMBONE CLASP: Found on European jewelry, primarily French, dating from the 1890s through the 1940s with sporadic use afterward.

EARLY SAFETY CATCH: One of the earliest safety catch mechanisms derived from those used in fine jewelry. As shown on an Edwardian filigree brooch, c. 1910-1915.

DRESS CLIP MECHANISM: This dress clip mechanism is a bit fancier than most, but its hinged mechanism works in the same way with prongs on the underside to hold the clip in place on a garment. Widely used in the 1930s, but some 1920s and 1940s examples exist as well. As shown on a 1930s rhinestone dress clip featured in Section One.

PIN CLIP MECHANISM: Double pronged pin clip is the manufacturer's name for this type of fastening mechanism, but collectors use the name "fur clip" more often. Used in the late 1930s and throughout the 1940s, although there was some lingering use into the 1950s. As shown on Eisenberg clips depicted in Section Two.

EARLY TUBE HINGE AND "C" CATCH

"C" CATCH

TROMBONE CLASP

EARLY SAFETY CATCH

DRESS CLIP MECHANISM

PIN CLIP MECHANISM

1930s PARROT CHATELAINE PINS

1930s SAFETY CATCH

MODERN HINGE MECHANISM

1930s PARROT CHATELAINE PINS: Dime store enameled pot metal parrot pins attached by a fine chain. These close with a more modern version of the "C" catch found on inexpensive jewelry from the 1930s on. **$35-$55**

1930s SAFETY CATCH: Akin to the modern safety catch, this one swivels to close around the pin stem. As shown on a 1930s pot metal brooch.

MODERN HINGE MECHANISM: First used in the 1890s and still found in modern jewelry design with slight variations. As shown on an Eisenberg Original brooch featured in Section Two.

NECKLACE CLASPS

Older spring ring clasps, usually found on jewelry dating to the early 1900s, do not have a nib to operate the spring. In the 1920s the nib was added, and this style of clasp has been used fervently since then.

Barrel clasps that unscrew into two parts usually date to the 1920s (see examples on 1920s necklaces shown in Section One) and 1930s, although they were used later in reproduction jewelry as well. Hidden clasps with a tongue that fit into a closure within a bead also came about in the 1920s and were used sporadically through the 1960s.

Hook and tail closures were popular from the late 1940s on, especially on beaded necklaces. Lobster claw clasps indicate modern jewelry made from the 1970s on, and they're seen on many items sold as "vintage style."

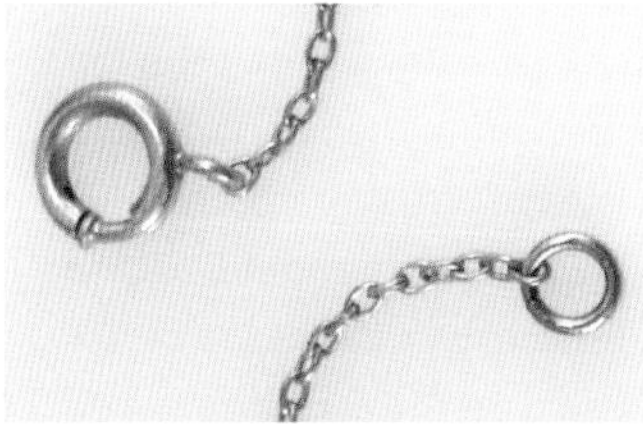

EARLY 1900s SPRING RING CLASP

HIDDEN BEAD CLASP

EARLY 1900s SPRING RING CLASP: The first spring ring clasps did not have nibs to make them easy to open like the versions from the 1920s on. As shown on the Edwardian filigree necklace depicted in Section One.

HIDDEN BEAD CLASP: Used on nicer strands of beads as early as the 1920s. As shown on a crystal beaded necklace from the 1930s.

FOLD-OVER CLASP: First used in the 1940s. As depicted on an early 1950s necklace.

TWO-PART BOX CLASP: Used on early jewelry through modern jewelry. As shown on a Christian Dior necklace dated 1970, depicted in Section Two.

HOOK AND TAIL CLOSURE: Popular in many different variations beginning in the 1950s. As shown on an early 1960s necklace.

LOBSTER CLAW CLASP: Widely used since the 1970s. As shown on a 1970s Christian Dior necklace featured in Section Two.

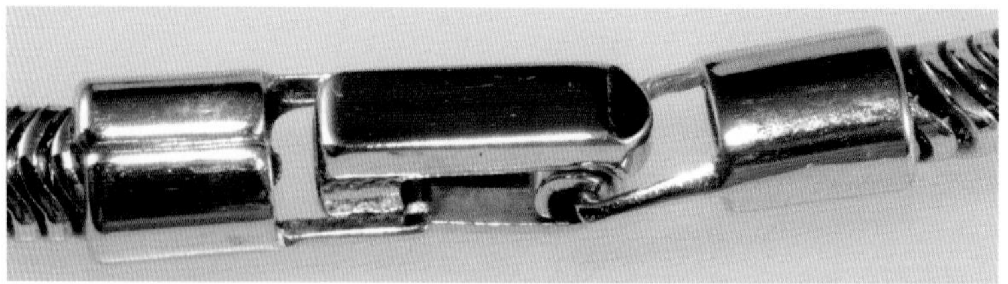

FOLD-OVER CLASP

TWO-PART BOX CLASP

HOOK AND TAIL CLOSURE

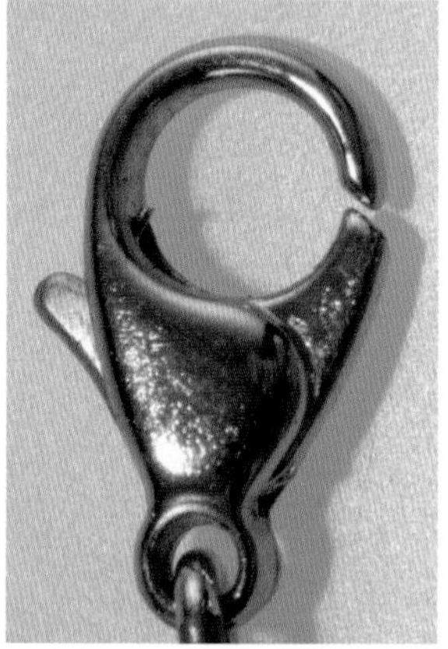

LOBSTER CLAW CLASP

EARRING FINDINGS

Early pierced earrings had fishhook wires, which changed to a kidney shape approaching the 1880s. Pierced earrings had threaded posts and screw backs in the Victorian era, but some thinner posts with a friction nut (similar to modern pierced earrings) were also made during this timeframe.

Screw backs were patented in 1894, and they gained wide use from the early 1900s through the 1940s with some carryover into the 1950s. Clip backs became popular in the 1940s and were used in different variations almost exclusively until the mid-1960s when pierced earrings came back into fashion. Brands like Miriam Haskell and Vendôme used a clever screw clip mechanism that allowed the tension to be adjusted on the ear for comfort.

VICTORIAN PIERCED EARRING

SCREW BACKS

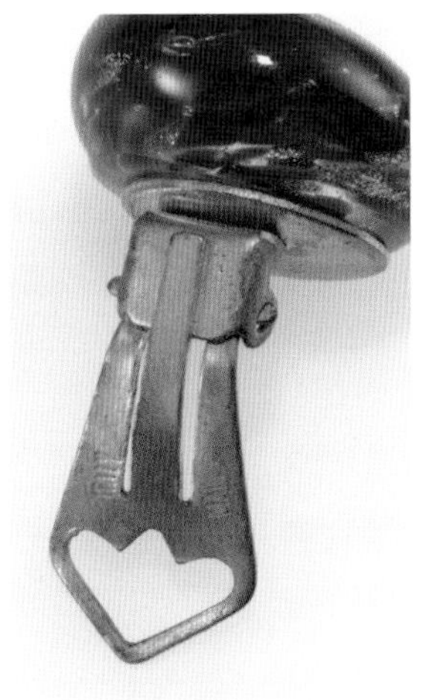

EARLY CLIP BACKS

AUSTRIAN CLIP BACKS

1950s CLIP BACKS

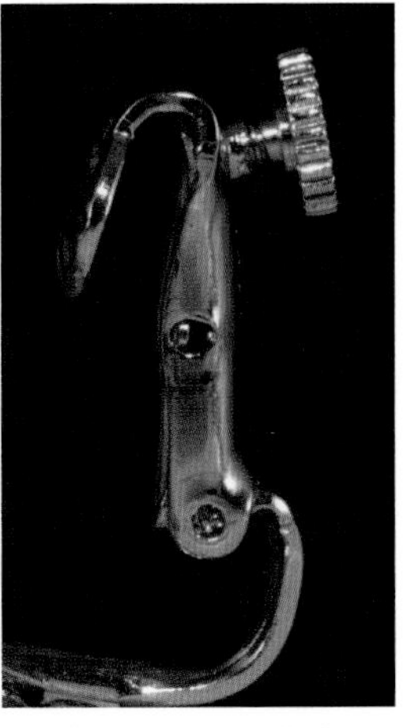

SCREW CLIP BACKS

VICTORIAN PIERCED EARRING: Threaded post with screw-on backs. Used through the early 1900s.

SCREW BACKS: Used from the mid-1890s primarily through the 1940s, although there were some earrings made with screw backs in the 1950s.

EARLY CLIP BACKS: The clip back shown is from a pair of Italian glass earrings dating to the 1930s. Brass clip backs used during the transition from screws to clips in the 1930s are often shaped like this or are more rounded on the clip.

AUSTRIAN CLIP BACKS: The clip back shown is a common style used on Austrian earrings dating to the 1950s.

1950s CLIP BACKS: From the late 1940s through the mid-1960s, clip earrings were the prevailing style. They fell out of fashion in the late 1960s when pierced earrings were once again in vogue. Similar clip backs have been used on jewelry since the 1960s as well.

SCREW CLIP BACKS: This type of finding was used in the 1950s and 1960s. It clips on the ear, but the screw allows for the tension to be adjusted for comfort.

Pierced earrings made from the mid-1960s through today offer a variety of findings. These range from smaller kidney wires (in comparison to mid-Victorian styles) to smooth posts with clutch backs.

Identifying Unsigned Jewelry

Learning to identify unsigned costume jewelry can be tricky, but it's also a great skill to cultivate. You'll be better prepared to save yourself some grief when you can pick out misattributed pieces, whether the seller is making an honest mistake or intentionally elevating the status of an item. And you'll know when to question a seller attributing jewelry to a particular brand if you just don't readily see the connection.

By learning to identify unmarked pieces, you'll open the door to some great finds you might otherwise overlook. These "sleepers," as they're known in the antiques business, are out there. You just need to learn to recognize them. And as a seller, you want to make sure you don't lose money by selling an unsigned piece too low. So where to begin?

First, it's important to understand that many pieces of jewelry were made by businesses known as "jobbers." These manufacturers took orders from jewelry distributors and made jewelry with the buyer's mark either molded into or affixed to the piece. That's why it's technically incorrect to refer to a piece known to be found with a number of different signatures, like the walrus brooch shown here, as designed by a specific person or company.

This piece only has a number (most likely a design number) impressed in the back, but it has been found with both Kenneth J. Lane and Hattie Carnegie placards affixed, making it impossible to attribute to one particular brand. It's also safe to say that neither of those people actually designed the piece. It was designed by a person who we may never be able to identify, who likely worked for the jobber rather than the brand doing the ordering, although that's not always the case. That's not to say you can't market a piece like this as unmarked, mentioning that it has been found with both these labels to substantiate the quality. It's a beautifully crafted example with lots of character.

Attributing unsigned jewelry is much easier in instances where pieces have been found and documented with signatures, or confirmed with documented research to have been made by a particular company. But there are instances where the signs are more obscure, and correctly attributing unsigned pieces is accomplished by paying attention to details relating to materials, manufacturing techniques, and construction. The following descriptions and photographs illustrate some of the telltale characteristics to keep in mind for a variety of brands and styles.

AUSTRIA AND SCHOFFEL

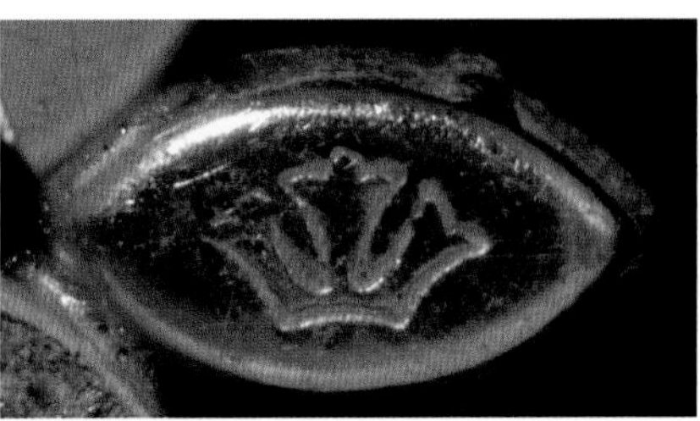
Schoffel crown mark, c. 1950s.

Schoffel pieces can be identified by a small crown mark found on the jewelry. Some of these marks can be rather obscure and easily overlooked. Many Schoffel pieces are also marked "Austria." Some pieces likely made by this Austrian company are completely unmarked, although the construction and overall styling becomes very familiar once you begin studying this jewelry.

The stones in these pieces are generally very high in quality and sparkle brightly – typical Austrian rhinestone brilliance. The style of clip backs used on Schoffel earrings, along with the findings and stone cups used on necklaces, bracelets, and brooches, provide clues along with the overall construction. The best way to learn to identify the construction of these unmarked pieces is by studying marked examples until they become completely familiar to you.

You will find on occasion that a piece marked "Austria" and "Made in Austria" does not resemble Schoffel's work. There were indeed other companies in Austria making jewelry in the 1950s and 1960s, and they also have dis-

Schoffel bracelet set, c. 1950s, alexandrite "color change" stones, which look blue or light purple depending on the light source, in gold-tone settings, with Schoffel crown mark. **$100-$125**

Jewelry courtesy of ChicAntiques.com

Schoffel necklace set, c. 1950s, purple cabochons with frosted clear navettes and aurora borealis accents in gold-tone metal, with Schoffel crown mark. **$225-$250**

Jewelry courtesy of ChicAntiques.com

Schoffel necklace set, c. 1950s, foiled cabochons surrounded by brown rhinestones, unmarked. Note the distinctive Austrian clip backs on the earrings and the style of the stone cups. **$150-$200**

Jewelry courtesy of ChicAntiques.com

tinctive findings, such as tiny ribbons of metalwork around the edges. Some of these can be found unmarked as well.

There's also a striking resemblance between the construction and components used in some Schreiner jewelry to that of a number of marked Made in Austria pieces, although a verifiable connection hasn't been documented.

BAKELITE

Bakelite was a very popular medium for jewelry manufacture in the 1930s, but getting the knack of identifying it doesn't come easy to everyone. Luckily, there are a number of techniques you can use to identify this plastic:

Sound Test – When Bakelite is worn, especially two or more bangle bracelets, it makes a distinctive clacking sound with the pieces tap together. Learning to recognize the sound of Bakelite is the easiest test to employ when you're shopping for jewelry.

Smell Test – Rub a piece of suspected Bakelite with your thumb until it begins to get hot and then quickly smell the heated area. If you notice a chemical odor, it's Bakelite. This test can also be accomplished with hot water, although that's not as convenient when you're away from home.

Simichrome Test – Simichrome is a type of metal polish that comes in tubes. If you put a small amount on the tip of a cotton swab and rub it on suspected plastic, a yellow residue should appear on the swab. Some black Bakelite does not respond to this test, however. This can also be accomplished with scrubbing bubble-type bathroom cleaners, but only the type that does not contain bleach. Sticking to Simichrome is safer. You can order Bakelite testing pads online; these are more portable and do the same trick quite well.

Also keep in mind that Bakelite fakes, what some people call "Fakelite," have widely infiltrated the vintage costume jewelry marketplace. Some of these items look very much like genuine Bakelite and even test like the real deal, so it's wise to buy from a reputable dealer if this is your area of interest. Confirmed fakes are indeed being marketed as genuine pieces (with no apparent repercussions) on a well-known multi-dealer website popular for marketing handmade jewelry as well as vintage items, and in other venues.

Other items newly carved of old Bakelite are available as well. Reputable Bakelite crafters will mark their jewelry as such, and these pieces are

ABOVE Face brooch, c. 1930s, applejuice and black carved Bakelite. **$100-$125**

Jewelry courtesy of ChicAntiques.com

LEFT Set of three bracelets, c. 1930s, two black and one orange matched Bakelite bangles. **$75-$100**

Jewelry courtesy of ChicAntiques.com

collectible in their own right. Some artisans who work in this medium are quite talented and have large followings.

BEAUJEWELS AND JUDY LEE

There are many overlapping characteristics of vintage jewelry marked Beaujewels and Judy Lee. This includes the heavily riveted construction, shape of the pin backs, similar earring backs on some pieces, and the type of stone cups used.

Unmarked pieces attributable to these brands are quite often confused with Juliana (DeLizza & Elster) due to the riveted construction. The number of rivets used to hold the components together is the first clue that these are not DeLizza & Elster, as there are more rivets incorporated in these pieces than those attributable to Juliana designs.

The v-shaped pin backs and the way they are attached, often using a pierced or filigree disc to decorate the back, is also a clue. The stones sometimes aren't quite as brilliant as those used in DeLizza & Elster designs, either, and they have more of a propensity to darken or discolor with age.

It's also interesting to note that matching sets are sometimes found with

ABOVE Brooch set, c. late 1950s, navette faux pearls with glass leaves and aurora borealis rhinestones, marked Beaujewels on earrings. **$65-$85**

Jewelry courtesy of ChicAntiques.com

RIGHT Large brooch set, c. 1950s, red and purple rhinestones in heavily riveted setting, unmarked, brooch 3 1/4" wide. **$100-$125**

Jewelry courtesy of ChicAntiques.com

marked earrings and an unmarked brooch. If you find a brooch you suspect to be Beaujewels or Judy Lee because of the intensely riveted back, search online for earrings to match, and you may be able to confirm your suspicion.

MIRIAM HASKELL

Since it's known that Miriam Haskell did not begin signing jewelry until after World War II, most of the pieces we find marked as such date to the late 1940s or newer. The jewelry made by Haskell prior to the war may have had some Haskell attributes such as faux pearls, bead clusters, and antiqued gold-tone findings, but many of these pieces look quite different from those collectors usually associate with this company, and the construction can also be vastly different.

This is especially true for Haskell pieces made during World War II when jewelry-making components were in short supply. While other makers were turning to sterling silver during this era, Haskell incorporated wood, shells, plastic, and fabric into the design and construction of jewelry, and all these pieces are unmarked.

For more information on identifying unsigned Miriam Haskell jewelry, *Miriam Haskell Jewelry* by Cathy Gordon and Sheila Pamfiloff is a recommended reference. Signed examples of Miriam Haskell jewelry are shown in Section Two.

LEFT Miriam Haskell dress clip, c. late 1930s, blue glass beads with brass findings and rhinestone dangles, 3 3/4" long. **$250-$350**

Jewelry courtesy of LinsyJsJewels.com

RIGHT Miriam Haskell brooch, c. 1940s, shell petals attached to plastic backing, 2 7/8" wide. **$65-$95**

Jewelry courtesy of ChicAntiques.com

ABOVE Miriam Haskell dress clip, c. 1940s, turquoise blue glass beads with brass findings and simulated pearls, 4" long. **$175-$225**

Jewelry courtesy of ChicAntiques.com

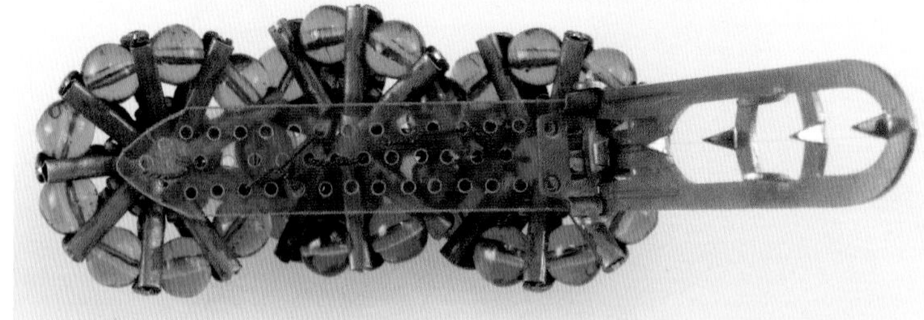

RIGHT Miriam Haskell dress clip, c. late 1930s, green glass bead clusters with rhinestone rondelles, 2 1/2" long. **$150-$200**

Jewelry courtesy of LinsyJsJewels.com

LEFT Miriam Haskell fur clip, c. late 1930s, glass leaves in pastel blue and pink, unmarked, 4" wide. **$250-$325**

Jewelry courtesy of LinsyJsJewels.com

ABOVE Miriam Haskell brooch, c. 1940s, red glass beads separated by rectangular metal spacers, 2 3/4" long. **$175-$225**

Jewelry courtesy of LinsyJsJewels.com

Miriam Haskell dress clips, c. 1940s, jewel-tone glass beads in sapphire, ruby, and emerald mounted to rhinestone pot metal leaves, marked "Made USA" on the clips, each clip 2 3/8" long. **$350-$475 pair**

Jewelry courtesy of LinsyJsJewels.com

JULIANA (DELIZZA & ELSTER)

When a group of collectors first put their heads together to compile the characteristics of unmarked jewelry they nicknamed "Juliana," a number of identifying factors were noted. Even before Juliana aficionado Cheryl Kilmer interviewed Frank DeLizza, one of the founders of the company, to get his initial input on this type of jewelry, collectors had already noted many features.

Some pieces with paper hangtags bearing the brand name "Juliana" had surfaced matching bracelets with a five link and band construction. Using those bracelets to piece together sets, construction techniques were pinned down. The author of this book first observed many of the pieces had heavy rivets unlike those seen in other styles of costume jewelry and contributed this observation to the conversation. Other characteristics have been confirmed and documented with the help of Mr. DeLizza.

Some DeLizza & Elster designs are easily recognizable by examining the stones and other components favored by this company. DeLizza & Elster used an abundance of specialty stones, including foiled and stippled cabochons and glass cameos. Many of its pieces incorporate dangling crystals or pearls, rhinestone balls, or foiled beads, as well as aurora borealis rhinestones as accents in many designs.

Many of the construction techniques unique to this company can be identified by examining the backs of its pieces: heavy rivets, link and band construction, stone cups, and soldering techniques including "figure eight" puddling.

DeLizza & Elster not only produced unmarked jewelry, it also served as a jobber for many other brands including Kenneth Jay Lane, Celebrity, and Hattie Carnegie. Refer to *Juliana Jewelry* by Katerina Musetti or *Juliana Jewelry Reference* by Ann Pitmann (now out of print but an e-book is available) for more information on jewelry made by this company.

To view additional jewelry examples, see Section Two under DeLizza & Elster's Juliana.

Juliana necklace, c. 1960s, clear rhinestones with foiled silver beads, rhinestone balls, and dangling crystals. Note use of dangling elements and heavy rivets. **$250-$300**

Jewelry courtesy of ChicAntiques.com

ABOVE Juliana brooch set, c. 1960s, brown and green bicolor molded glass stones with brown, gray, and aurora borealis accents. **$175-$225**

Jewelry courtesy of ChicAntiques.com

LEFT Juliana set, c. 1960s, foiled cabochons with brown rhinestones and matching glass bead dangles. Back view shows DeLizza & Elster's five link and band construction. **$175-$225**

Jewelry courtesy of ChicAntiques.com

Juliana brooch set, c. 1960s, round Vitrail Medium III dark stone surrounded by green and aurora borealis rhinestones. Note open-backed center stone, heavy rivets, and figure eight puddled soldering. **$225-$250**

Jewelry courtesy of ChicAntiques.com

Juliana spray brooch, c. 1960s, green, blue, and purple rhinestones with aurora borealis accents. Note spray style and open-backed navettes. **$125-$150**

Jewelry courtesy of ChicAntiques.com

Juliana necklace, c. 1960s, clear rhinestones with dangling simulated pearls and crystal beads. Note abundant dangles and heavy rivets on back construction. **$325-$400**

Jewelry courtesy of ChicAntiques.com

ABOVE Juliana crystal bead bracelet, c. 1960s, clamper-style bracelet with clear rhinestones and crystals. Note the four heavy rivets and engraved design on the metalwork. **$125-$150**

Jewelry courtesy of ChicAntiques.com

RIGHT Juliana necklace set, c. 1960s, peacock blue and teal green rhinestones. Note the open-back navettes and rhinestone chain dangles. Earring backs have been converted to pierced in this set. **$225-$275**

Jewelry courtesy of ChicAntiques.com

BELOW Juliana brooch, c. 1960s, oval foiled glass cabochons surrounded by gray rhinestones. Note ring construction and figure eight puddled soldering on back. **$125-$150**

Jewelry courtesy of ChicAntiques.com

Juliana necklace set, c. 1960s, brown rhinestones with aurora borealis accents and dangling crystals. Note the open back settings, heavy rivets, and crystal bead dangles. **$525-$600**

Jewelry courtesy of ChicAntiques.com

MARNER

Marner of Providence, Rhode Island, founded in 1946 and eventually solely owned by Julio Marcella, produced high quality costume jewelry and jewelry components including lampwork glass heart-shaped stones patented in 1956.

These stones were used in jewelry with Marner's own branding marked most often Jewels by Julio or Julio Marcella, according to an article by Cheri Van Hoover on MilkyWayJewels.com. They were also used in pieces Marner jobbed for other brands, such as Kramer and Hattie Carnegie; Carnegie was its best bead customer.

The glass stones are seen in a variety of colors: varying shades of pink, blue, black, amber, and green, some with swirls of sparkly copper (like those shown here) and having a similar look to Venetian aventurine beads. In an interview with Julio Marcella's nephew, Van Hoover verified the business closed its doors in 1957, so jewelry made by Marner using these stones will date to the mid-1950s. However, vintage advertising dating to 1962 clearly shows Hobé jewelry marketed as "Mayorka Petals" using these stones patented by Marner. It's not clear how Hobé came to use them after Marner's closing, but it is evidence that other companies used them sporadically in later designs.

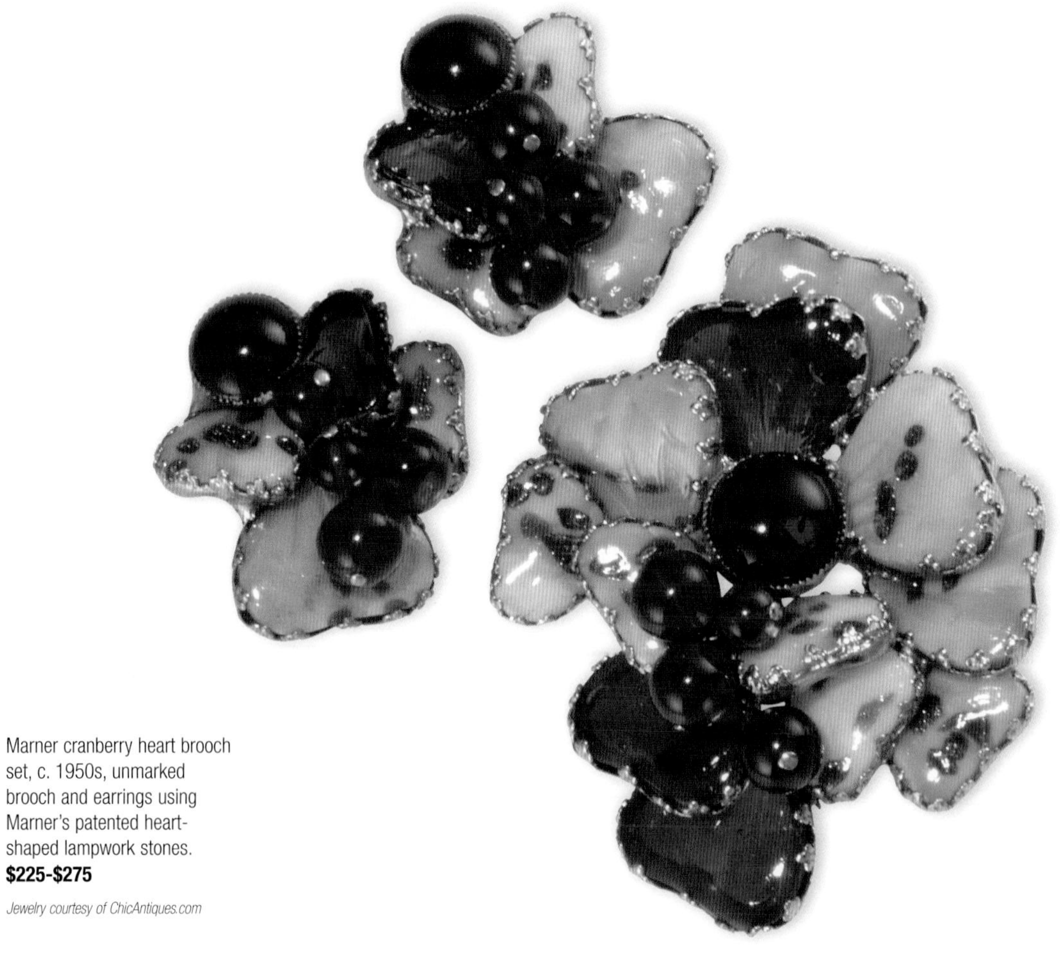

Marner cranberry heart brooch set, c. 1950s, unmarked brooch and earrings using Marner's patented heart-shaped lampwork stones.
$225-$275

Jewelry courtesy of ChicAntiques.com

REGENCY

Regency jewelry has a distinctive look that most collectors learn to recognize very quickly even before turning the piece over to examine it for a mark. Some pieces are unmarked, however, especially earrings, which have sometimes been confused with other unsigned pieces made by brands such as Juliana by DeLizza & Elster, and Schreiner on occasion.

Most unsigned Regency styles can be identified by matching them to other similar pieces that are marked, and some styles are actually quite common. Many have dark gold-tone plating or matte plating in either silver- or gold-tone coloring. This brand was also known for using molded glass leaves,

LEFT Regency pearl flower set, c. 1950s, unmarked earrings with marked brooch, baroque pearls with clear rhinestones, and antiqued silver-tone findings. **$135-$165**

Jewelry courtesy of LinsyJsJewels.com

BELOW Regency set, c. late 1950s, unmarked earrings with marked brooch, foiled glass cabochons with green and yellow rhinestones. **$225-$275**

Jewelry courtesy of LinsyJsJewels.com

ABOVE Regency set, c. late 1950s, unmarked earrings with marked brooch and bracelet, purple art glass cabochons with purple and aurora borealis rhinestones. **$300-$375**

Jewelry courtesy of LinsyJsJewels.com

BELOW Regency set, c. late 1950s, unmarked earrings with marked brooch, red glass drops with red and aurora borealis rhinestones. **$135-$165**

Jewelry courtesy of LinsyJsJewels.com

foiled cabochons, art glass teardrop stones, and an abundance of colorful Austrian rhinestones. The finish on these pieces is frequently worn, but the stones are more often than not very brilliant.

SCHIAPARELLI

Schiaparelli earrings are almost always marked on the clip back. Most bracelets and necklaces usually have a signature plaque as well. But, as you can see through these illustrations, there are exceptions.

Early pieces dating to the 1930s have a lowercase block letter mark when they are signed. Later pieces made after 1949 have script lettering.

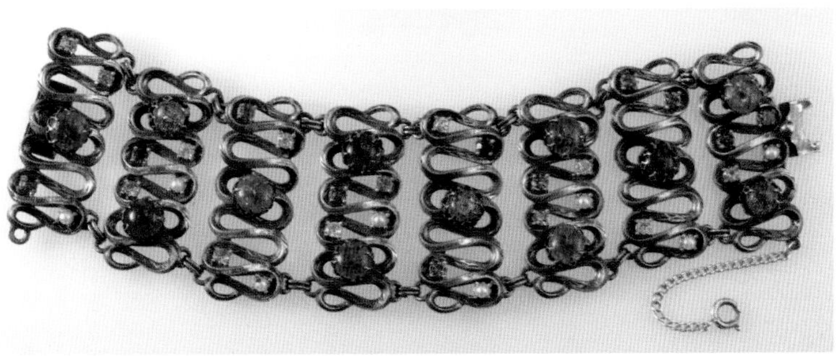

Schiaparelli multicolor parure, c. 1950s, unmarked necklace with signed bracelet and earrings, cabochons in bright hues with matching accent stones and petite faux pearls. **$825-$900**

Jewelry courtesy of LinsyJsJewels.com

Schiaparelli set, c. 1950s, single marked earring with unsigned necklace and bracelet, purple oval rhinestones surrounded by clear accents. **$450-$525**

Jewelry courtesy of ChicAntiques.com

Schiaparelli "watermelon" set, c. 1950s, unsigned necklace with marked earrings, "watermelon" or Vitrail Medium II navette rhinestones in silver-tone settings. **$1,100-$1,300**

Jewelry courtesy of LinsyJsJewels.com

Some pieces, however, were only marked with "Shocking" pink torso-shaped paper tags that were discarded with wear. So while the earrings may have a mark, a matching bracelet or necklace will not. It's interesting to note that of all Schiaparelli jewelry made after 1949, brooches are found unsigned more often than other pieces.

Since Schiaparelli jewelry is not overly common, perusing signed pieces in online selling venues is one of the best ways to become familiar with the overall look of these designs and learn the typical characteristics of them. Whether marked or unmarked, pieces often incorporate large unfoiled rhinestones, "lava rock" stones, leaf- and shell-shaped stones, brightly colored cabochons, and/or vividly hued beads. See Section Two of this book to view more signed examples.

SCHREINER

Schreiner of New York is associated with many pieces of unmarked jewelry. Some of them are easy to identify once you've handled them simply because the same settings were used again and again. Others are unique but still have attributes of note that point to Schreiner.

As shown in the photos here, one of the most obvious construction techniques Schreiner fans learn to look for is the hook and eye found by examining the backs of these pieces. This company is also known for its incredibly beautiful art glass stones and beads and high quality glass pearls in intricately crafted pieces (refer to Section Two of this guide for more examples). Schreiner also

Schreiner brooches, c. 1950s, unsigned coral stones in gold-tone metal and signed blue version of the same brooch in silver-tone metal. This style was made in a variety of colorations. **$125-$225 each**

Jewelry courtesy of ChicAntiques.com

ABOVE Four Schreiner brooches, c. 1950s, red, amber, yellow, and clear versions of the same Schreiner collage design. Only the amber version shown top right is marked Schreiner. **$250-$350 each**

Author's Collection

RIGHT Schreiner dangle brooches, c. 1960s, simulated turquoise and white versions of the same articulated 5 3/4" design. Only the turquoise version is marked Schreiner New York. **$300-$350 each**

Author's Collection

Schreiner earrings, c. 1950s, marked Pat. Pend., ear clips with clear rhinestones in gunmetal settings, backs have "donut hole" clips frequently found on marked Schreiner earrings. **$75-$95**

Jewelry courtesy of ChicAntiques.com

Schreiner brooch and necklace, c. 1950s, amber and yellow rhinestone brooch marked Schreiner with unmarked coordinating necklace, both in dark copper-tone settings. Note the hook rigidly soldered in place on the necklace. This is typical construction on many Schreiner necklaces. See more examples under Schreiner in Section Two. **$275-$325**

Author's Collection

Schreiner brooch, c. 1950s, signed Schreiner New York, gray unfoiled cabochons with matching inverted rhinestones. Back construction shows hook and eye construction. This style was made in a variety of colors in both signed and unsigned versions. **$225-$275**

Jewelry courtesy of ChicAntiques.com

Schreiner ovoid brooches, c. 1960s, amber/green and coral/green rhinestone brooches using the same setting. This style was made in many different color combinations and were both signed and unsigned. **$250-$300 each**

Jewelry courtesy of ChicAntiques.com

Schreiner cluster brooch, c. 1950s, fuchsia rhinestones, faux pearls, and aurora borealis accents in gold-tone metal. Back construction shows use of riveted clusters along with hook and eye construction. **$225-$275**

Jewelry courtesy of ChicAntiques.com

Schreiner cluster brooch set, c. 1960s, unsigned set featuring art glass cabochons with white and copper-colored rhinestones in a gold-tone setting. Back construction shows use of riveted clusters along with hook and eye construction typical of Schreiner. Matching earrings have "donut hole" clip backs. A similar set was made with the Sherman mark (see aurora borealis illustrations for example) and different earring backs. **$225-$275**

Jewelry courtesy of ChicAntiques.com

Schreiner collage brooches, c. 1950s, yellow and multicolor rhinestone brooches in matching collage styles. Only the yellow version is marked Schreiner New York. **$225-$275 each**

Jewelry courtesy of ChicAntiques.com

used dogtooth prongs and crimped stone cups in many of its designs, but many other companies did as well.

So, while you can certainly learn to skillfully attribute unsigned pieces as Schreiner, it's important to bear in mind that no single characteristic makes an attribution. You must look at the entire piece as a whole, as well as examine individual components, when evaluating this jewelry to avoid confusing it with Juliana, Sherman, and other well-known brands.

SELRO

Paul Selenger founded Selro in the late 1940s and produced jewelry that was evidently popular in the 1950s and 1960s because many different styles have been documented and they come up for sale frequently. Many of these items were not marked – they were sold on paper cards or with hangtags, which were removed after they were purchased – although some do have a Selro or Selini signature. On rare occasions they have both marks.

Some of the company's necklaces, bracelets, and earrings are more recognizable than others, namely those featuring an Asian woman (sometimes referenced as Asian princess or Thai Girl when marketed, although not all of them are wearing Thai headwear) or an Asian man (often referenced as a Noh mask or devil). The female faces came in a variety of colors, but white, black, and red are the most common. The male faces can be found in turquoise blue, red, yellow, and white. This type of jewelry was made in more limited quantities featuring African faces as well, and there were other similarly styled lines.

Metalwork on unmarked Selro jewelry is usually heavy and molded with lots of texture to enhance the chunky style of the designs. Confetti Lucite in various colors, shapes, and sizes was used by this company, as were pierced elements with an Asian influence in colors beyond the traditional simulated jade. Some pieces are embellished with a smattering of rhinestones or faux pearls as well.

Bolo-style necklaces (which don't actually adjust like a true bolo tie) with many different forms of embellishment were also a prolific item of manufacture for Selro, but the company also made other necklaces with chunky elements linked together. Those necklaces dating to the 1950s and 1960s often can be found in sets with large matching bracelets measuring as wide as two inches.

There are many different types of jewelry made during the 1950s and 1960s that look similar to Selro. Some contain Lucite elements or have five-station bracelet construction, and most of these are unmarked. They do, however, have telltale differences in the components and construction when examined closely. Marketers who either don't know any better or simply don't care often present them as Selro and/or Selini without doing research. Visit http://imageevent.com/themanyfacesofselro/ to see a wide selection of Selro jewelry examples.

Selro simulated tortoise bracelet, c. 1950s, brown plastic with amber rhinestones in gold-tone metal, unmarked.
$100-$125

Jewelry courtesy of ChicAntiques.com

Selro Lucite set, c. early 1950s, purple confetti Lucite set in bolo-style necklace, wide five-station bracelet and screw back earrings, unmarked.
$225-$275

Jewelry courtesy of ChicAntiques.com

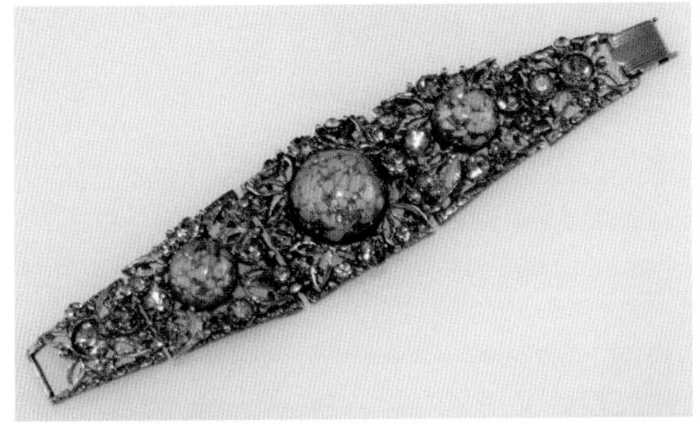

LEFT Selro Asian woman necklace, c. 1950s, black and red Asian faces set in silver-tone metal, unmarked. **$125-$150**

Jewelry courtesy of ChicAntiques.com

ABOVE Selro Lucite bracelet, c. 1950s, light purple confetti Lucite cabochons with coordinating rhinestones in heavy gold-tone setting, unmarked. **$175-$200**

Jewelry courtesy of ChicAntiques.com

Selro earrings, c. 1950s, green plastic cabochons with pink rhinestones in gold-tone metal screw back settings, unmarked. **$25-$35**

Jewelry courtesy of ChicAntiques.com

Schiaparelli dangle earrings, c. 1950s, brown, pale pink, and pale yellow kite-shaped stones in dangle two-part mounting, marked Schiaparelli, 2 1/2" long. **$300-$350**

Jewelry courtesy ChicAntiques.com

BIBLIOGRAPHY

This list of books was not only referenced as research material for this guide, but are also titles the author would suggest to anyone wanting to learn more about vintage costume jewelry:

American Costume Jewelry Art & Industry, 1935-1950: Volumes A-M and N-Z by Carla and Roberto Brunialti (Schiffer)

Answers to Questions About Old Jewelry by Jeanene Bell (Krause Publications)

Collecting Costume Jewelry 202 by Julia C. Carroll (Collector Books)

Copper Art Jewelry: A Different Lustre by Mathew Burkholz and Linda Lichtenberg Kaplan (Schiffer)

Costume Jewelry for Haute Couture by Frances Müller (Vendôme)

European Designer Jewelry by Ginger Moro (Schiffer)

Fashion Jewelry: The Collection of Barbara Berger by Harrice Simmons Miller (Assouline)

Jewelry of the Stars by Joanne Dubbs Ball (Schiffer)

Juliana Jewelry by Katerina Musetti (Schiffer)

Juliana Jewelry Reference by Ann Pitman (Collector Books)

Miriam Haskell Jewelry by Cathy Gordon and Sheila Pamfiloff (Schiffer)

Monet: The Master Jewelers by Alice Vega (Schiffer)

The Napier Co. by Melinda Lewis (Life by Design Institute)

Official Price Guide to Costume Jewelry by Harrice Simmons Miller (House of Collectibles)

Warman's Jewelry Identification & Price Guide, 5th Edition by Christie Romero with introduction by Pamela Y. Wiggins (Krause Publications)

Additional Online Resources Utilized for Research:

Antiques at About.com – www.antiques.about.com

Costume Jewelry Collectors International – www.costumejewelrycollectors.com

Guyot Brothers Jewelry History – www.guyotbrothers.com

Knoll & Pregizer Jewelry by Robin Deutsch – http://imageevent.com/nibor56/knollpregizer

Milky Way Jewels – www.milkywayjewels.com

Morning Glory Antiques Jewel Chat – www.morninggloryjewelry.com/jc/JewelChat.htm

Researching Costume Jewelry – www.illusionjewels.com

The Many Faces of Selro – http://imageevent.com/themanyfacesofselro/

INDEX

LEFT Star sapphire rhinestone bracelet, c. 1950s, simulated star sapphire cabochon surrounded by sapphire and ice blue rhinestones decorating silver-tone hinged cuff bracelet, unmarked, 1 1/4" wide. **$95-$125**

Jewelry courtesy ChicAntiques.com

LEFT Juliana brooch, c. 1960s, oval "Easter egg" stippled cabochon center stone surrounded by brown, green, orange, and aurora borealis rhinestones. Note use of "Easter egg" (a collector's nickname) stone, heavy rivets, and figure eight puddled soldering. **$325-$400**

Jewelry courtesy of ChicAntiques.com

Q

R

S

T

U

V

W

Y